If You're So Ethical, Why Are You So Highly Paid?

Ethics, Inequality and Executive Pay

Alexander Pepper

LSE Press

Published by
LSE Press
10 Portugal Street
London WC2A 2HD
press.lse.ac.uk

Text © Alexander Pepper 2022

First published 2022

Cover design by Diana Jarvis

Print and digital versions typeset by Siliconchips Services Ltd.

ISBN (Paperback): 978-1-909890-94-7
ISBN (PDF): 978-1-909890-95-4
ISBN (EPUB): 978-1-909890-96-1
ISBN (Mobi): 978-1-909890-97-8

DOI: https://doi.org/10.31389/lsepress/eth

This book has been peer-reviewed to ensure high academic standards. For full review policies, see https://press.lse.ac.uk

Suggested citation:
Pepper, A. 2022. *If You're So Ethical, Why Are You So Highly Paid? Ethics, Inequality and Executive Pay.* London: LSE Press. DOI: https://doi.org/10.31389/lsepress/eth
License: CC BY-NC

To read the free, open access version of this book online, visit https://doi.org/10.31389/lsepress/eth or scan this QR code with your mobile device.

Contents

Extended contents

Preface

One of my friends, let's call her 'Mrs Taylor', used to run the elementary department of an independent boys' school in the south of England. She is an enlightened teacher and, as well as ensuring that her pupils had a good grounding in English, maths and science, she also ran a lunchtime philosophy club to introduce year 1 and year 2 boys (aged between five and seven) to, as she used to describe it, the 'joys of philosophising'. Each week they would discuss knotty dilemmas such as the pros and cons of factory farming, the significance of names, and the problems of perception (why do our eyes sometimes deceive us?). As is often the case with philosophy, the boys learnt that there is typically no single right answer to a philosophical question, just a set of better or worse possible responses and a clearer understanding of the problem.

One day Mrs Taylor presented her class with the following scenario. 'Imagine,' she said, 'that we are a band of pirates. By our efforts we have recently uncovered an enormous stash of treasure. After celebrating our find, we now have to decide how we are going to share out the treasure. I am the leader of the pirate band, so I will get half the cash. You have to decide how to share the other half out among yourselves.' The boys discussed a number of options, perhaps sharing out the treasure in proportion to their ages, how good they were at football, or based on their academic ability. After some discussion they decided to share the treasure equally – the egalitarian option. This seemed to be a satisfactory conclusion, but there was one thing that still troubled one member of the class. 'Excuse me, Mrs Taylor,' said one little boy cautiously, 'why is it that you get half the treasure?'

'Why does Mrs Taylor get half the treasure?' or 'Is it fair that some people appear to obtain a disproportionate share of income and wealth?' has become one of the defining issues of our age. The particular focus of this book is on business executives, the people Thomas Piketty in *Capital in the Twenty-First Century* describes as 'super-managers'.[1] It is a book about distributive justice, about how the benefits and burdens of economic activity are shared out among individuals in society. More prosaically, therefore, the 'Mrs Taylor' question might be restated as follows:

> Is it right in terms of distributive justice that super-managers appear to be able to capture such a large share of the value created by the companies that they manage?

Everyone seems to have a view about this question. The left-leaning High Pay Centre asks whether it is right that by the third or fourth working day of the year the average chief executive of a FTSE 100 company will earn as much as the average UK worker will earn in a year.[2] The right-leaning Adam Smith Institute has argued that outrage over executive pay is over-egged, and that the falling pay gap between FTSE 100 CEOs and their employees in 2020 and 2021, largely driven by challenging economic circumstances during the worst months of the COVID–19 pandemic, was nothing to celebrate – it did not help the economy or make the average worker any richer.[3] The Investment Association, the trade body and industry voice for UK investment managers, has called for companies to be sensitive to the experiences of employees and customers when deciding on executive pay and bonuses.[4] The Archbishop of Canterbury, Justin Welby, has warned that Britain faces a 'crisis of capitalism', citing growing public anger about excessive executive pay and arguing that our 'form of capitalism has lost any contact with a moral foundation'.[5] However, what nobody has done before is to explore what business executives themselves think about distributive justice. How do their personal beliefs about justice and fairness fit with high rates of executive pay? Are top executives really the greedy ethical egoists of popular culture, or do they share wider society's concerns about large pay differentials and high levels of inequality? If so, how do they reconcile their ethical beliefs with high pay? These are the kinds of questions that I have set out to explore in this book.

The purpose of this book

I have been thinking about senior executive pay for over 30 years. From 1990 to 2008 as a partner at PwC I advised companies on tax and executive compensation. For the last 14 years as an academic at LSE I have taught a course on strategic reward and carried out research on the pay and motivation of senior executives. In academic terms I am something of a magpie – I like collecting and reassembling diverse ideas from different academic disciplines. I was educated first as a philosopher, then (because the careers service at my first university pointed out that there were very few jobs for philosophers) as an accountant, and most recently as a management scholar (itself, at least in my case, an eclectic mix of new institutional economics, organisational behaviour and economic psychology). Part of the attraction of studying executive pay is that it has allowed me to dabble in economics, psychology, law, accounting and most recently business ethics. Politically

I am a socially inclined ('modern', 'American' or 'left', depending on your choice of terminology) liberal. My intellectual heroes include Thomas Jefferson, John Dewey, John Maynard Keynes, Karl Popper and John Rawls. I believe in free markets, free trade, individual rights, capitalism, democracy and internationalism, but also in equal opportunities, equality before the law, and social justice – I am committed to the idea that everybody has the right to lead a dignified life. I have been concerned for some time about inflation in executive pay, which I believe is a problem for a number of reasons. First, executives may be extracting economic rents (that is, amounts exceeding that which is economically or socially necessary) to the detriment of shareholders and other stakeholders who have a legitimate interest in the financial performance of companies. If so, this is inefficient and results in suboptimal economic outcomes. Second, differential rates of pay inflation in the last 30 years (high rates of pay inflation for executives compared with moderate rates for others) have contributed to rising levels of inequality – this is Thomas Piketty's argument, which I consider in Chapter 1. Third, high executive pay has resulted in public outrage that, if unchecked, might lead in the course of time to social unrest. Each one of these is sufficient cause for governments, investors and executives to be concerned.

My main objective in writing this book is to try to extend the debate about executive pay – to move it on from the economics and public outrage which seems to characterise much of the current debate – by introducing a philosophical perspective and some ethical terminology. Although it draws on academic research, in particular a paper entitled 'What Do Business Executives Think about Distributive Justice' which was first published in the *Journal of Business Ethics* in September 2020,[6] it is intended for the widest audience possible, including business executives, investors, policymakers, and the public generally. For this reason, all references have been confined to endnotes. I hope the book will also be of interest to academics in the disciplines of philosophy and economics, as well as social scientists who have an interest in the topical issue of high pay. Readers in the policy area will find the arguments relevant, particularly given the fact that high levels of executive pay are a frequent source of public concern and political debate.

Finally, readers who are familiar with the literature on distributive justice will recognise that *If You're So Ethical, Why Are You So Highly Paid?* is a riff on the title of a book by the Oxford philosopher G.A. Cohen, *If You're an Egalitarian, How Come You're So Rich?* I hope if he were still alive to read this that he would not be offended.

—Alexander Pepper
Guildford, May 2022

Acknowledgements

I owe particular thanks to my research collaborators on the project which lies behind this book, Dr Susanne Burri, who taught me about distributive justice, and Dr Daniela Lup, who helped with the statistics. The appendix to the book draws on published joint work with them. Adam Bassett, Jason Buwanabala, Tom Gosling and Simon Hunt of PwC also played significant roles in the original research.

My thanks are also due to a number of 'critical friends' who have read and commented on various drafts of the manuscript. These include my colleague Rebecca Campbell, Stefan Stern, formerly director of the High Pay Centre, Alistair Pepper (the family economist) and Robert Pepper (the family philosopher). Simon Pepper gave advice on the title. Particular thanks are due to Dr Susanne Burri and Professor Paul Willman, who both made some especially insightful suggestions on the main text. A number of anonymous reviewers have also generously given up their time to read and comment on the manuscript. If I have forgotten anyone, I hope they will forgive me. All errors or omissions of course remain my own.

About the author

Alexander ('Sandy') Pepper is Emeritus Professor of Management Practice at the London School of Economics and Political Science, where he has been teaching and researching since 2008. Prior to this he had a long career at PricewaterhouseCoopers, where he held various senior management positions, including as global leader of PwC's Human Resource Services consulting practice from 2002 to 2006. His research and teaching interests include organisations and management theory, with a particular focus on the theory of the firm, corporate governance, and business ethics. Sandy is one of the UK's recognised experts on executive pay. He is the author of several academic articles and books on the subject,including *Agency Theory and Executive Pay* (2019), *The Economic Psychology of Incentives* (2015) and *Senior Executive Reward – Key Models and Practices* (2006), as well as numerous blogposts and newspaper articles.

List of figures

Glossary

While this book is intended to be non-technical and for a wide audience, some economic and philosophical terminology has inevitably crept in. As far as possible, I have explained any technical terms I have used as part of the main narrative. For convenience, I also include a short summary here.

Desert: This is an important concept in ethics and the theory of justice; it means what is *deserved*, taking into account all relevant principles of justice and fairness. Desert requires each person to be provided with benefits and burdens proportionately, taking into account their relative contribution.

Distributive justice: One aspect of the philosophical theory of justice is how economic *goods* (see the separate definition below) should be distributed in society. *Distributive justice* focuses on securing just or fair outcomes. This is sometimes contrasted with *procedural justice*, which focuses on the processes and procedures whereby particular outcomes are determined.

Efficiency: *Efficiency* is a foundational concept in economics. An economically *efficient outcome* is one where inputs are minimised for a given level of outputs, or outputs are maximised for a given level of inputs. 'Pareto efficiency', named after the Italian economist and philosopher Vilfredo Pareto, provides that an outcome is efficient only if no one can be made better off without making somebody else worse off.

Egalitarianism: An ethical perspective that emphasises the desirability of economic, political and social equality.

Egalitarians prioritise equality for all people and take it as axiomatic that all humans are equal in fundamental worth or moral status.

Epistemology: The branch of philosophy that enquires into the nature and grounds of knowledge. *Epistemology* addresses fundamental questions such as 'what can we know?' and 'how do we know it?'.

ESG investing: An investment approach that involves the consideration of environmental, social and governance factors alongside financial measures in the investment decision-making process.

Good: In economics, a *good* is a noun meaning a thing of value – 'any physical object, natural or manmade, or service rendered, that could command a price in a market'. In ethics, on the other hand, the *good* is a normative concept, meaning 'that which conforms to the moral ideal'. For example, Plato defines 'the good' in his theory of forms as 'a perfect, eternal, and changeless entity existing outside space and time, in which particular good things share'. The philosopher John Rawls also talks about 'social goods', such as freedom and equal opportunities, which he saw as more fundamental to leading a good life.

Isomorphism: In sociology, *isomorphism* describes a process whereby social practices or entities come to develop similar structures or forms. Sociologists distinguish between *mimetic isomorphism* (copying or imitation), *coercive isomorphism* (for example, complying with a mandated rule), and *normative isomorphism* (such as following 'best practice').

Long-term incentive plan (LTIP): Also known as an 'LTIPs', *long-term incentive plans* involve contingent awards of deferred shares that vest over time (normally at least three years) provided that demanding performance conditions, typically relating to financial performance, are met. LTIP awards are normally only made to very senior executives and are dependent on their continuing employment. LTIPs are intended to align the interests of top managers with those of shareholders.

Maximin: In game theory, *maximin* is the strategy that seeks to maximise the minimum possible payoff of any player in the game. In the hands of the philosopher John Rawls, the maximin strategy becomes a principle of justice that he calls 'the difference principle'. This requires that any inequality in society should only permitted if, in the long-run, it benefits the least well-off member of that society.

Prisoner's dilemma: A foundational concept in the economic theory of games, describing a situation in which it pays two or more individuals to behave in a particular, suboptimal way, even though it would benefit them collectively to act in a different way.

PwC: PricewaterhouseCoopers, one of the 'big four' global accounting firms.

Rent: *Economic rents* are payments made to a factor of production (land, labour or capital) in excess of that which is necessary to bring that factor into production, for example a scarcity rent for goods in short supply.

Restricted stock award (RSA): An award of shares with a time-base vesting schedule, typically of at least five years. *Restricted stock awards* are much simpler than LTIPs, and do not include performance conditions, but may require shares to be held for a further period after vesting.

Stocks and flows: Economists distinguish between the *stock of goods* measured at a particular point in time, and the *flow of goods* measured over a period of time. Thus, wealth is a stock, while income is a flow.

Sufficientarianism: The ethical perspective that all members of society should have an income that is sufficiently high to lead a dignified life, and that this is the only principle of distributive justice that matters.

Thought experiment: Philosophers sometimes use *thought experiments* – imagined, extreme, hypothetical situations, which often appear to be somewhat detached from reality – to test, from first principles, their ideas, concepts, theories and ethical doctrines.

Welfare: An important concept in economics and ethics, *welfare* is an assessment of the wealth, health, happiness and general well-being of any individual or group of people.

Value: In economics, *value* means something of worth. This is sometimes further subdivided into either 'value in use', being the pleasure or welfare that a commodity generates for its owner, or 'value in exchange', being the quantity of other commodities (or more usually money) for which something can be exchanged. In ethics, *value(s)*, more often discussed in the plural, are the basic and fundamental beliefs that guide or motivate attitudes or actions. Values help to determine what is important to us. They are personal qualities that we choose to embody to guide our actions.

CHAPTER 1

Introduction – ethics, inequality and executive pay

> To study a corporation may be economics, or sociology, or law; to study its activities as resulting from the purposes of persons or as affecting the welfare of persons, and to judge its acts as good or bad from such a point of view, is ethics.
>
> John Dewey and James Hayden Tufts (1908)[7]

Why do some people appear to obtain a disproportionate share of income and wealth? The French economist Thomas Piketty, in his book *Capital in the Twenty-First Century*, frames the problem in a rather old-fashioned way as a tussle between capital and labour. His main thesis is that inequality is rising because the rate of return on capital, held disproportionately by the wealthy, exceeds the rate of growth of output and income. It did this at the end

How to cite this book chapter:
Pepper, A. 2022. *If You're So Ethical, Why Are You So Highly Paid? Ethics, Inequality and Executive Pay.* London: LSE Press. Pp. 1–17.
DOI: https://doi.org/10.31389/lsepress/eth License: CC BY-NC

of the 19th century and is doing it again at the beginning of the 21st. As a result, according to Piketty, 'capitalism automatically generates arbitrary and unsustainable inequalities that radically undermine the meritocratic values on which democratic societies are based'.[8] This is, he believes, a most serious matter. It is hard to think otherwise.

A brief history of inequality in the 20th century

Inequality can be measured in a number of different ways, depending on whether the focus is on wealth, savings or income. Income inequality is illustrated by charting the top 1 per cent of the population's share of total income. For Anglo-Saxon countries such as the US and UK, over the course of the 20th century this distribution shows a distinct 'U' shape: the level of inequality was very high at the start of the century and fell to much more moderate levels in the 1970s, before rising again in the 1990s and at the start of the 21st century.[9]

The end of the 19th century in the US is described by historians as 'the Gilded Age', a satirical reference, after Mark Twain's book of the same name, to the gilding of economic success that benefitted one section of the population but which masked widespread deprivation affecting other parts of the population. For sociologists of the period it was a pejorative term describing a time of materialistic excess combined with extreme poverty.[10] The journalist and historian Simon Heffer has described the corresponding period in Britain as 'The Age of Decadence'.[11] On the European continent it is known as 'La Belle Époque' ('the beautiful era').[12]

The Gilded Age gave way to the 'Progressive Era' in the early 1920s, when Presidents Theodore Roosevelt, William H. Taft and Woodrow Wilson, supported by investigative journalists such as Ida Tarbell and progressive lawyers like Louis Brandeis, challenged the industrial 'trusts' created by wealthy and powerful businessmen like Cornelius Vanderbilt, John D. Rockefeller and Andrew Carnegie, who established monopolies over railroads, oil refining and steel production, aided by financiers such as J.P. Morgan and Andrew Mellon. At the same time, social reformers like Jane Addams lobbied hard to improve the conditions of the working classes and to reduce poverty.

Despite the best efforts of the progressive movement, by 1920, towards the end of Woodrow Wilson's presidency, the top 1 per cent still earned around 19 per cent of total income. However, as a result of continuing social reform in the US, Franklin D. Roosevelt's New Deal Coalition, which defined modern liberalism throughout the middle third of the 20th century, as well as the rise of the Labour Party in the UK and the great economic levelling effect of the Second World War, by 1975 this had reduced to 10 per cent in the US and 7 per cent in the UK.

Changes in governments and new economic policies, especially 'Reaganism' in the US and 'Thatcherism' in the UK, meant that the top 1 per cent's share of total income began to rise again in the mid-1980s. By the beginning of the 1990s some commentators were talking about the start of a 'Second Gilded Age'.[13] Others trace the origins of the new era back to Milton Friedman's contention in the *New York Times* in 1970 that 'the social responsibility of business is to increase its profits'.[14] This was followed in 1976 by a much-cited paper entitled 'Theory of the Firm: Managerial Behavior, Agency Costs and Ownership Structure' by economists Michael Jensen and William Meckling, who described corporations as 'legal fictions which serve as a nexus for a set of contracting relationships among individuals' and provided support for linking executive pay to rises in company share prices.[15] These intellectual foundations were followed in turn by the demerger movement of the 1980s, when investment banks took apart many large conglomerates in the US and UK, arguing – often, it has to be said, with some justification – that the sum of the parts was greater than the whole. What finance scholars have described as the 'market for corporate control' (meaning that underperforming management teams could be replaced) forced companies to restructure en masse, with waves of redundancies and outsourcing that left the corporate sector 'lean, mean, and focused on its core competencies'. Sociologist Greta Krippner describes this whole process as 'the financialization of the economy'. As another sociologist, Jerry Davis, puts it, '[t]he corporation has increasingly become the financially-oriented nexus described by its theorists'.[16]

As is clear from the above, neither Krippner nor Davis is a fan of financialisation. The merits or otherwise of the fundamental shift in industrial and economic policies that began with the Reagan and Thatcher governments in the 1980s are not really the subject of this book. It must also be remembered that the 1970s, when inequality was least pronounced, was a traumatic economic decade in the US and the UK, with low growth, high unemployment, high inflation, and poor returns for investors. Nevertheless, one of the consequences of financialisation is that by 2020 the top 1 per cent's share of total income had again reached 19 per cent in the US and 13 per cent in the UK, as shown in Figure 1.1.

Lest this be thought solely an Anglo-Saxon phenomenon, at the start of the 20th century the levels of inequality in Germany and France were similar to those found in the US and UK. In 1920 the top 1 per cent earned 22 per cent of total income in Germany and 18 per cent in France. By 1975 this had reduced to 10 per cent in Germany and 8 per cent in France. The rise in the top 1 per cent's

Figure 1.1: Income inequality in the US and UK, 1920–2020

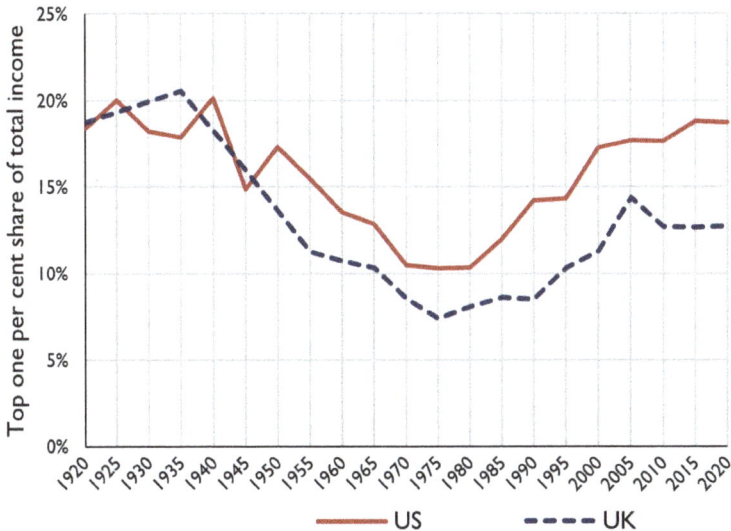

share since then has been less steep than in Anglo-Saxon countries, and by 2020 had reached 13 per cent in Germany and 10
per cent in France. In Sweden the top 1 per cent earned 22 per
cent of total income in 1920, 9 per cent in 1975 and 10 per cent
in 2020. Even communist China, with its distinctive political and
economic systems, saw the top 1 per cent's share of total income
rise steadily from around 6 per cent in the 1970s to nearly 14 per
cent by 2020.

The rise of the super-manager

In explaining the rise in income inequality in the latter part of the
20th century and beginning of the 21st, Piketty draws particular attention to the increasing inequality of labour income, which
he attributes to two things – the growing wage gap between college graduates and school leavers, and the rise of the very highly

Figure 1.2: Ratio of CEO total earnings to employee average earnings, 1965–2020

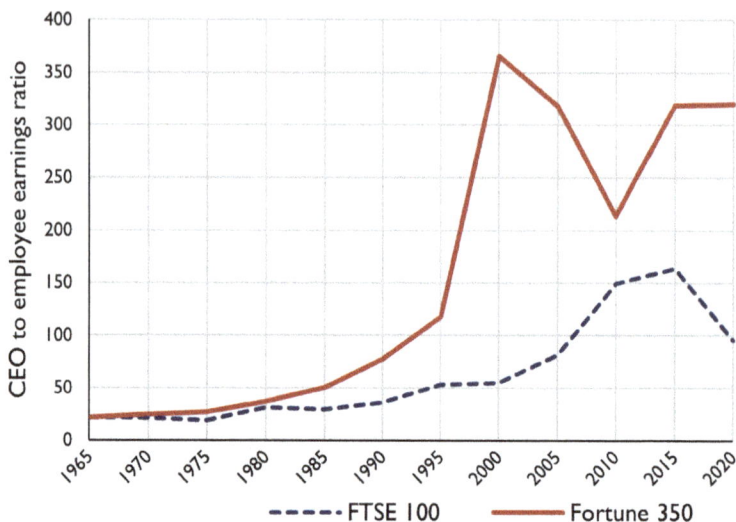

paid 'super-manager'. Nobel Prize-winning economist Robert Solow writes that 'it is pretty clear that the class of super-managers belongs socially and politically with the rentiers'.[17] This is a reference to 'rentier capitalism', structured around the exploitation of financial capital and other scarce assets at the expense of wage earners. It is the rise of the highly paid super-manager and the question of distributive justice that is my primary concern in this book.

Figure 1.2 charts the ratio of median CEO total earnings to all-employee average earnings for the period 1965–2020 for FTSE 100 companies in the UK and Fortune 350 companies in the US. At the start of the period the ratio of median total pay of FTSE 100 CEOs to UK average national private sector earnings was 22:1 and the ratio of Fortune 350 CEOs to US typical worker earnings was almost the same, at 21:1. In the US the ratio peaked in 2000 at 366:1, falling to 213:1 in 2010 after the global financial crisis, before rising again to 320:1 by 2020. In the UK the ratio peaked in 2015 at 163:1 and appeared to be stabilising at around 135:1, before declining steeply to 95:1 in 2020 during the COVID–19 pandemic, when executive pay fell sharply. In 2020 median FTSE 100 CEO pay amounted to £2.7 million, compared with UK average national private sector earnings of just over £28,000, though most commentators attribute the fall from the 2019 level of £3.25 million to financial constraints imposed as a result of the economic consequences of the pandemic. Fortune 350 CEO median pay was $20 million in 2020, compared with a typical worker's earnings in the US of around $65,000.[18]

CEO compensation and the ratio of CEO pay to average earnings in Germany tends to be lower than in the UK, and is lower still in Sweden, but data for France are broadly comparable to the UK. German companies tend to pay higher salaries than in the UK or France, but deliver smaller amounts in the form of stock-based pay. All these countries have seen significant rates of growth in executive pay between 2000 and 2020.[19]

'Super-managers' are the focus of this book, and the question that I pose is an ethical one: is it right in terms of distributive justice that super-managers appear to be able to capture such a large share of the value created by the companies which they manage?

Ethical enquiry

Academics can at times be extraordinarily tribal. Each discipline and sub-discipline has its own journals, favours different research methodologies, and prefers to attend conferences with other practitioners of the same discipline. In 1973 the economist Axel Leijon-hufvud wrote a delightful satirical essay entitled 'Life Among the

Econ', describing the economics profession as through the eyes of an imaginary anthropologist observing a tribal community 'in the far North'. He notes that the 'Econ' tribe was marked by clannishness and xenophobia, with particular 'distrust and contempt' for the 'Polscis' and 'Sociogs'.[20] Nor are political scientists (Polscis) or sociologists (Sociogs) exempt from this kind of tribalism.

While economists, political scientists, sociologists, jurists and management scholars have all written extensively about executive compensation and inequality, they have tended to talk among themselves rather than to each other. In this book I draw on research from across the social sciences, but do so from a perspective strongly influenced by my original training as a philosopher, on the grounds that, as the quotation from Dewey and Tufts at the beginning of this chapter makes clear, the actions of persons associated with corporations, and whether they are to be judged good or bad, is ultimately a matter of ethics.

This book crosses traditional boundaries in another respect as well. Until recently philosophers have eschewed empirical work, preferring rational analysis, dialogue in seminars and at conferences with other philosophers, and thought experiments. Social scientists favour an empirical approach, using surveys, field observation and experiments in behavioural laboratories to gather information, before analysing the data using statistical techniques. This study combines both approaches.

One of the most famous philosophical thought experiments is the so-called 'trolley problem'. Imagine a scenario in which a runaway train is hurtling down a hill towards a group of children who are playing on the track below a railway bridge. Is it permissible to push a grown man off the bridge in order to stop the train and save the children if no other options are available? Many books and academic papers have been written on this subject.[21] Thought experiments are used to place logic and reason at the heart of ethical decision-making. They are used to test the validity of ethical principles in particularly tricky cases (does the application of a specific principle make intuitive sense?) as well as to test the ethical relevance of particular features of a case (what happens when one feature is varied while others are held constant?). Many philosophers think thought experiments are of critical importance in developing robust ethical understanding.[22]

Philosophers use carefully constructed scenarios in their thought experiments. For example, the American philosopher John Rawls asks us to imagine ourselves in the 'original position', behind a 'veil of ignorance' in which we rationalise our conceptions of right and wrong devoid of any prior knowledge about our ability, ethnicity, gender or position in society. Rawls describes the original position in the following terms.

> This original position is not, of course, thought of as an actual historical state of affairs, much less as a primitive condition of culture. It is understood as a purely hypothetical situation characterized so as to lead to a certain conception of justice. Among the essential features of this situation is that no one knows his place in society, his class position or social status, nor does anyone know his fortune in the distribution of natural assets and abilities, his intelligence, strength, and the like. I shall even assume that the parties do not know their conceptions of the good or their special psychological propensities. The principles of justice are chosen behind a veil of ignorance. This ensures that no one is advantaged or disadvantaged in the choice of principles by the outcome of natural chance or the contingency of social circumstances.[23]

In this way, by imagining ourselves stripped of any natural advantages and knowledge of our position in the world, Rawls hopes to turn us into objective moral arbiters, capable of reaching a consensus about the most just way of doing things. There should be no disagreements about ethical principles behind Rawls's veil of ignorance. You will hear more about John Rawls in subsequent chapters.

John Dewey, the American pragmatist, believed that thought experiments were especially important in the field of ethics. As the Canadian philosopher Cheryl Misak says, when writing about Dewey's approach to ethical enquiry, through thought experiments, 'we learn something about ourselves, how we will react in certain moral scenarios, and if we try on other people's shoes, we can learn something about how those others might react'.[24] Later on you will hear more about John Dewey as well.

Although ancient philosophers like Plato and Aristotle were interested in the passions as well as reason, and in moral behaviour as well as ethical reasoning, in the last two centuries analytical philosophers have tended to leave behavioural investigations to social scientists. Since the turn of the 21st century, a new movement of *experimental philosophy* has returned to the ancient philosophical tradition, asking questions about how human beings actually happen to be, and accepting that this involves the study of phenomena that are messy, contingent, and context-dependent.

In order to shed some light on the question of executive pay and inequality, I decided to take a thought experiment into the field, to encourage senior executives from around the world to think deeply about how corporate income is shared, in much the same way that Mrs Taylor took a similar thought experiment into the classroom.

The 'is–ought' problem

Many philosophers and most social scientists point to a logical gulf between the beliefs that people hold as a matter of fact and the beliefs that they ought to hold. The 18th-century Scottish philosopher David Hume argued that positive statements about what is the case and normative statements about what should be the case are logically different – you cannot easily move from one to the other. This is known as the 'is–ought' problem. It is similar in many ways to the distinction between facts and values. Most social scientists and many philosophers take the statement 'you cannot get an ought from an is' as a truism, but is it in fact true? By delving in the murky depths of what people actually believe, might we not be able to discover important clues about what should be the case?

Most philosophers subscribe to a long-held theory that knowledge is 'justified true belief'. If all three conditions (justification, truth and belief) are met, then we can claim that we have knowledge. If this epistemological principle (epistemology is the branch of philosophy concerned with the theory of knowledge) is correct, then ethical statements that satisfy the justified true belief formula might be regarded as ethical knowledge. If so, then it is entirely plausible that examining facts about people's actual beliefs might give important clues as to what might constitute ethical knowledge (that is, justified true beliefs).[25] The relationship between ethical knowledge, ethical beliefs and ethical behaviour is illustrated in Figure 1.3. Activities comprising A and B both involve some kind of causal mechanism (albeit an iterative one in the case of the activities connecting ethical knowledge and ethical beliefs). We can assume that these mechanisms are capable of being investigated. While B is primarily the

Figure 1.3: The knowledge–beliefs–behaviours nexus

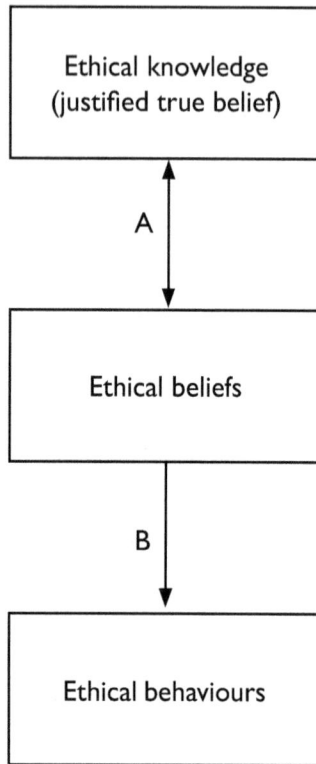

```
┌─────────────────────────────┐
│  Ethical knowledge          │
│  (justified true belief)    │
└─────────────────────────────┘
               ↑
             A │
               ↓
┌─────────────────────────────┐
│                             │
│  Ethical beliefs            │
│                             │
└─────────────────────────────┘
               │
             B │
               ↓
┌─────────────────────────────┐
│                             │
│  Ethical behaviours         │
│                             │
└─────────────────────────────┘
```

domain of psychology and the social sciences, A falls within the domain of philosophy, especially within the field of experimental philosophy. The job of the philosopher becomes at least in part one of 'sorting out' our underlying beliefs to ensure that the deep structure is logical, coherent and warranted. By examining actual beliefs and straightening them out to ensure that they are logical and coherent, we can gain important clues about ethical knowledge.

The Oxford political philosopher David Miller, who we will meet again in Chapter 6, argues that social scientific and philosophical studies of justice are necessarily inter-dependent. He puts it like this:

> I maintain that empirical evidence should play a significant role in justifying a normative theory of justice, or to put it another way, that such a theory is to be tested, in part, by its correspondence with our evidence concerning everyday beliefs about justice.

He goes on:

> The aim is to achieve an equilibrium whereby the theory of justice appears no longer as an external imposition conjured up by the philosopher, but as a clearer and more systematic statement of the principles that people already hold.[26]

There are a lot of 'ifs' in this first argument. So let me advance two further lines of thought in order to justify my method of enquiry. The second argument begins with a proposition. Let us for the moment accept that distributive justice is an important component of social justice, and is necessary to cement social order. Social order is most likely to be maintained if the general populace believes that there is a significant measure of distributive justice in society. Common opinions about what constitutes distributive justice must somehow therefore be incorporated into our ethical theory. The criteria that the philosopher uses to determine truth from falsehood must, broadly speaking, be the same as those used by the ordinary person – the notion that philosophers can discover 'truth' in some other way would seem to be hard to justify. This approach is known as 'pragmatism', made famous at the end of the 19th century by three Americans: Charles Sanders Peirce, William James and John Dewey. In very broad terms, pragmatism is a philosophical tradition in which it is understood that knowing the world is inseparable from agency within it.

Philosophical concepts should be tested by scientific experimentation. Philosophical enquiry must contribute to social progress, otherwise it is of little value. John Rawls's approach to justice theory also owes something to this. He is concerned that valid principles of justice must be publicly defendable – the people who are going to use them must be able to justify them to one another using commonly accepted modes of reasoning.

This second argument will also be resisted by some scholars – not everyone agrees with the pragmatists' approach. Even so, there is a third argument which I believe provides strong support for my method. It goes like this: if, as we will see to be the case in due course, executives advocate principles of distributive justice that are consistent with the best normative theories (that is, theories accepted by at least some modern philosophers as corresponding to the highest principles of ethical reasoning), as well as public opinion generally, but the behaviours which we see exhibited in the world are not consistent with the principles that the executives have advocated, then there are very strong reasons to challenge their behaviours.

Commentators on both the left and the right might still take issue with my approach. They might contest the sample selection – why draw only from the population of 'senior executives' rather than from the public as a whole? They might argue, on the one hand, that the phenomenon of very highly paid executives is an inevitable consequence of corporate power and a failure of capitalism. Or they might argue, on the other hand, that high pay is an entirely justified consequence of free market economics. I argue differently – that many investors, directors and executives recognise that high pay and inequality are problematic and unsustainable, even if they appear to be unable to stem pay inflation. For all these reasons, even if executives are not morally neutral, their opinions are nevertheless important.

Some definitions

This book is about distributive justice – how are the benefits and burdens of economic activity to be shared out among individuals in society? – or, to put this another way, what constitutes a just allocation of goods in society? A 'just allocation' might mean 'equality' – everybody gets the same. It might mean 'desert' – outputs are proportionate to inputs, so that there are rewards for effort. It might mean 'sufficiency' – all members of society should have an income that is sufficiently high to lead a dignified life. It might mean some combination of these, or something else altogether. 'Goods' may be provided in the form of money or in kind. (We must set aside for the time being the question of whether some goods may be intrinsic – such as truth and beauty, which are pursued for their own sake – rather than extrinsic – such as money, which is pursued because of what it might help us to obtain.)[27] Goods might be thought about in terms of what economists call 'flows', arising over a period of time, which we shall call 'income', or as 'stocks' existing at a particular point in time, which we shall call 'wealth'. 'Economic rents' are payments made to a factor of production (land, labour or capital) in excess of that which is necessary to bring that factor into production. This contrasts with producer surplus or normal profit, both of which involve productive human action. In labour markets, rents are amounts paid over and above the market clearing wage. An 'efficient' outcome is one where inputs are minimised for a given level of outputs or outputs are maximised for a given level of inputs. 'Pareto efficiency' (named after the Italian economist and philosopher Vilfredo Pareto, 1848–1923) goes further and provides that an outcome is efficient only if no one can be made better off without making somebody else worse off. A 'Pareto improvement' can only be achieved if someone is bettered and no one is harmed in the process. It follows that multiple Pareto efficient outcomes are possible and that these cannot be ranked by the Pareto criterion, a problem we will return to in Chapter 4. 'Society' can be thought about at various different levels – within companies (for example, how profits are shared between shareholders, executives and other employees), within countries (how gross domestic product is shared among citizens) or between countries (such as how wealth is shared between the developed and the developing world). 'Distributive justice' refers primarily to just outcomes as opposed to just processes – we typically talk about the latter in terms of 'procedural justice'. A just outcome may be the result of a just process but could equally well arise by accident. A just process may lead to a just outcome but does not necessarily do so – hidden information might mean that the people presiding over the process inadvertently ignore certain factors which might be pertinent to a just outcome.

To sum up

In this chapter I have stated my main question – is it just that super-managers appear to be able to capture such a large share of the value created by the companies that they manage? I have explained that this is essentially an ethical question, and hence that I am going to draw upon the analytical philosopher's toolkit to trying to answer it. I have explained how, working with colleagues, we used an experimental approach to the question, investigating the beliefs of over a thousand business executives to see if this provided knowledge about distributive justice that might be of some practical use in a world in which it is generally recognised that there is widespread inequality. In the next chapter I begin my enquiry in earnest.

CHAPTER 2

Executive pay and distributive justice

I begin this chapter by examining three approaches to academic work on executive pay – optimal contracting theory, the managerial power hypothesis, and the market failure approach. I then expand on the concept of distributive justice, briefly describing six different ways in which distributive justice has been thought about by philosophers.

The economics of executive pay

According to standard economic theory, welfare is maximised when a worker is paid their marginal product, the value that they personally create, which in turn is dependent upon their skills and is also connected with the levels of supply and demand for their services. Therefore, so the economic argument goes on,

How to cite this book chapter:
Pepper, A. 2022. *If You're So Ethical, Why Are You So Highly Paid?: Ethics, Inequality and Executive Pay.* London: LSE Press. Pp. 19–37.
    DOI: https://doi.org/10.31389/lsepress/eth License: CC BY-NC

highly experienced senior managers, who are in short supply and whose services are in high demand, warrant high wages in line with the marginal contribution they make to firm profits. If, for example, during a CEO's tenure, some supporters of high executive pay might argue, he or she presides over a substantial increase in shareholder value, then why should they not be rewarded by receiving a proportion of that increase? However, when it comes to top managers, standard economic theory faces three problems. First, there is the measurement problem: how do you calculate the marginal product of a top manager, as opposed to, say, a machine operator working on piecework, and over what period of time? Is an increase in shareholder wealth (a combination of dividends and capital gains) really a good measure of a CEO's contribution? Second, there is the problem of team production: how do you measure the contribution of an individual to a team, for example a top manager to a company's top management team? Although the CEO is a key decision-maker and important figurehead, many people in a company contribute to the creation of shareholder value. The third problem is that labour markets for highly experienced top managers are not very efficient, as I will explain. Accordingly, there is a risk of what economists call 'market failure' – rewards may be far higher than the market clearing wage that is necessary to obtain the services of appropriately qualified executives.

Optimal contracting

In order to address these problems, economists developed agency theory, first linked with executive compensation in the 1970s in a famous article that was written by American economists Michael Jensen and William Meckling. They postulated that, in order to motivate executives (agents) to carry out actions and select effort levels that are in the best interests of shareholders (principals), boards of directors, acting on behalf of shareholders, must design incentive contracts that make an agent's compensation contingent on measurable performance outcomes. A related economic framework known as 'tournament theory' extends the agency model by proposing that principals structure a company's management hierarchy as a rank-order tournament, thus ensuring that the highest-performing agents are selected for the most-senior management positions. It predicts that compensation is an increasing convex function of an agent's position in the management hierarchy – imagine a graph with seniority on the x-axis, pay on the y-axis, and the line mapping the relationship between the two variables curving upwards with an increasing gradient. The rise in remuneration between levels in the hierarchy varies inversely in proportion to the probability of being promoted to the next level. As a result, the compensation of the CEO, ranked highest in the tournament, will typically be substantially more than the compensation of executives at the next highest level. This way of conceptualising executive pay, bringing together agency and tournament theories, is now generally referred to as 'optimal contracting theory'.[28]

The main problem for optimal contracting theory is that empirical evidence gathered over the past 35 years has failed to establish a statistically significant link between executive pay and a firm's financial performance, which agency theory predicts should be the case. In 1990 Michael Jensen and Kevin Murphy were unable to find a strong statistical connection between CEO pay and performance.[29] Ten years later, Tosi, Werner, Katz and Gomez-Mejia concluded that incentive alignment as an explanatory agency construct for CEO pay was at best weakly supported by the evidence, based on their meta-analysis of over 100 empirical studies.[30] Most economists now appear to accept that the strongest empirical correlation is between executive pay and firm size, not between executive pay and financial performance as predicted by agency theory. Baker, Jensen and Murphy have even called this 'the best documented empirical regularity regarding levels of executive compensation'.[31]

The managerial power hypothesis

An alternative approach, most closely associated with the American legal scholar Lucien Bebchuk, is that CEOs have too much power over boards of directors. Compensation contracts are not negotiated at arm's length because, given the prevalence of social networks among executives and directors, board members align more closely with the CEO than with shareholders. Top managers use their power to influence the level and structure of their pay, thus extracting rents – value over and above the rewards that they would have received under optimal contracting. The absence of arm's-length bargaining results in excessive levels of executive pay and weak pay-for-performance relationships. This approach is widely known as the 'managerial power hypothesis'.[32]

Bebchuk and his various co-authors back up the managerial power hypothesis with two subsidiary propositions. The first of these is the existence of 'outrage costs', anger and upset caused to outsiders, and the consequential social costs and reputational damage that might be done to a corporation and its directors if an executive's compensation arrangements goes far beyond what could be justified under optimal contracting. The second proposition is that companies structure executive compensation plans in such a way that the extraction of rents is 'dressed, packaged, or hidden – in short, camouflaged' in order to mitigate outrage costs.

The problem with the managerial power approach is that it is very difficult to verify, despite the researchers' best efforts to put forward testable predictions. A review by Carola Frydman and Raven Saks of US executive compensation data covering the period 1936 to 2005 concluded that neither agency theory nor the managerial power hypothesis was supported by the available evidence.[33]

The market failure approach to executive pay

A third approach to academic work on executive compensation, which I have pioneered and which inevitably therefore I favour, is predicated on the inefficiency of executive labour markets. According to standard economic theory, an efficient market requires many buyers and sellers, homogenous products (or at least good substitutes), free market entry and exit, plentiful information, and little economic friction (any factors that inhibit the free operation of the market). The problem with the market for top executives is that practically none of these conditions holds good. At any one time only a few top jobs may be open, and only a limited number of suitable candidates may be available. No two senior executives are the same, and information about them is far from perfect. Information about prices (what executives are paid) has historically been far from perfect too, despite the best endeavours of governments and regulators over the past 10 years. Finally, all sorts of legal, tax and accounting factors impact on the way senior executives are paid and the types of contracts companies choose to enter into with them. According to this thesis, inflation in executive pay is an example of market failure. I call this approach to executive compensation, for rather obvious reasons, the 'market failure hypothesis' or the 'market failure approach to executive pay'.

The remuneration committee's dilemma

A possible explanation for the market failure hypothesis is that companies face a prisoner's dilemma when it comes to chief executive officers' pay. To demonstrate this, let us assume that all CEOs are paid broadly equal amounts, with only marginal variations in pay, justifiable by reference to job size, industry, specialist expertise and so on. Assume also that, in the available population of CEOs, 20 per cent are superior to the others and would, if they worked for your company, increase the value of the firm by more than the average. On the other hand, 10 per cent are inferior to the others and would, if you employed them, potentially reduce the firm's value. If all companies offered modest remuneration, then it would be in the interests of an individual company to defect and pay over the odds. By doing so they might attract top talent and, potentially, be more successful than their competitors. Conversely, a company would not want to find itself in the position of paying significantly below average. To do so might mean it could only attract inferior chief executives. No one will congratulate a company's remuneration committee for its financial prudence if the result is a second-rate management team. Thus, offering higher salaries is the dominant strategy, even though by doing so companies will generally be no better off than if they all paid modest salaries. On the other hand, this is better than risking being in the bottom 10 per cent. I call this 'the remuneration

Figure 2.1: The remuneration committee's dilemma

		Company G, H, I and J	
		Pay average	Pay over the odds
Company F	Pay average	Second best for F, G, H, etc., = α	Best for G, H etc., worst for F = β
	Pay over the odds	Best for F, worst for G, H, etc., = δ	Third best for F, G, H, etc., = γ

committee's dilemma'. Figure 2.1 represents the dilemma in diagrammatic form for a firm 'F' competing for a new CEO with firms 'G', 'H', 'I' and 'J'.

The four quadrants in Figure 2.1 are labelled 'α', 'β', 'γ' and 'δ', moving clockwise from top left to bottom right. The payoffs for firm F are ordered $\delta > \alpha > \gamma > \beta$. The first quadrant, α, is the best overall result for firms F, G, H, I and J and the second-best result for any one company (as it is paying no more than is necessary and facing the same odds as all other companies – a one in five chance of getting one of the best CEOs and one in 10 chance of getting one of the worst). The second quadrant, β, is the worst for firm F as it gets the worst CEO by paying low while everyone else pays over the odds. The fourth quadrant, δ, is the best result for firm F as it is more or less guaranteed to get one of the best CEOs by paying high while everyone else pays low. The third quadrant, γ, is the third best option for everyone – all companies pay over the odds while facing the same odds as in the first quadrant. But this also appears to be the equilibrium point – technically, the 'Nash equilibrium' – the best response for any company given the strategies of the other companies.

The investors' collective action problem

A second possible explanation for the market failure hypothesis is that the failure to act by investors is a specific example of the general theory of groups advanced by the American economist and political scientist Mancur Olson in the 1960s. The fact that executives exercise management and control over large corporations and are able, on occasions, to further their own interests at the expense of investors, might be recognised as a collective action problem. A large corporation is in a way a kind of quasi-public good to its members. They all derive benefits from the corporation, but individual self-interested action will not secure those benefits.

Collective action problems often relate to the elimination of a cost, which constitutes a good to those who would otherwise bear that cost. There is a sense in which the earnings of a corporation are a collective good to investors, so that an investor owning a small percentage of total stock is like any member of what Olson calls a 'latent group', with no incentive to challenge the management of the company as the costs of doing so are likely to outweigh the potential benefits.[34]

Minority shareholders in public companies have reasonable expectations of receiving regular dividends and periodic capital gains, in excess of safer alternative forms of investment and proportionate to the level of risk they are taking. While it is in the interests of shareholders to monitor the activities of managers, they will wish to do so at minimal cost. They will certainly wish to avoid incurring monitoring costs that materially eat into their income and gains. While a £3.25 million bonus paid to the CEO of a FTSE 100 company might seem a lot of money, to a large investment management firm with £50 billion of assets under management, holding, say, 1 per cent of the company's shares, the amount involved is relatively trivial, especially if the question is about whether the CEO's bonus is 10 or 20 or even 30 per cent higher than it should be. Investors have historically been prepared to accept rent-seeking behaviour by managers as long as their reasonable expectations of income and gains are met.[35] I call this 'the investors' collective action problem'.

The long-term incentive plan (LTIP) valuation issue

A third potential reason why CEO pay in the UK and US has increased so much more rapidly than average earnings may be the delivery mechanism. All-employee average earnings predominantly reflect payments made in cash, and track inflation. A significant proportion of CEO pay, on the other hand, is delivered in shares and tracks stock price indices: in 2020 75 per cent of Fortune 350 CEOs' pay was realised in stock; in the UK the equivalent proportion was 51 per cent. When it comes to increases in FTSE 100 CEO pay, the strongest correlation is with annual increases in the FTSE 100 share price index, especially if you ignore the years in which the index falls. Average earnings and CEO pay are in part linked to entirely different asset classes.[36]

Not only do they track different indices but people attach different values to different classes of asset. If you were to offer an executive £1,000 in cash or a share-based performance-related financial instrument with an economic value of £3,000, do not be surprised if the executive would prefer to take the cash. By the time they have applied subjective probability-based discounts for uncertainty and complexity of around 17 per cent and time discounts in excess of 30 per cent per annum, the psychological value that the executive attaches to the financial instrument may be as little as somewhere between 25 and 30 per cent of its economic value.[37] A consequence of paying people with an asset they do not fully value is that they want more of it in order to compensate for their subjective 'loss'. Hence it seems entirely reasonable to conjecture that companies increase the size of long-term incentive plan (LTIP) awards to executives to compensate them for the perceived loss of value when compared with less risky, more certain, and more immediate forms of reward.[38] This is what I mean by 'the LTIP valuation issue'.

The remuneration committee's dilemma, the investors' collective action problem, and the LTIP valuation issue are not mutually exclusive – all three effects may be at work. None of them is easy to solve through conventional means, although in Chapters 8 and 9 I will turn to potential solutions – where ethics come back in.

Distributive justice

While the economic arguments discussed above are important, economic efficiency is not the only benchmark against which to judge the appropriateness of incentives. A philosopher would argue that we also need to consider the ethical standards of justice and fairness. How might the high pay of top managers be justified from an ethical perspective?

In medieval times, markets and economic exchange were regarded as being embedded in a broad set of social institutions and ethical norms. Usury – lending money at immoderate interest – was wrong, but labour was entitled to be compensated for its efforts. A just price was generally regarded as being one that ensured that neither party was able to exact unfair gains at the expense of the other. In ancient Greece, Aristotle had advanced the notion of 'compensatory justice', which preserved equity in exchange, understood as an arithmetic proportion shared out around a mean. Medieval philosophers like Thomas Aquinas, the scholastics, or 'schoolmen', as they were known, built upon this idea with the concept of a 'just price'. When it came to labour, a just wage was the market price, provided that monopoly or fraud had not upset the mechanism of the market. However, the scholastics also recognised that in thin markets, when there were limited numbers of buyers and sellers, or in cases of shortages or economic necessity, the agreed price did not necessarily reflect the just price, and other factors had to be considered in determining whether the exchange price was fair.[39]

Some senior executives and remuneration committees will argue that rich executives are entitled to their wealth: they have earned it by presiding over the generation of profits and increases in shareholder value. But for their efforts this additional wealth would not have existed. In any case, shareholders have voluntarily agreed to transfer some of their wealth to the senior executives who are their agents. They are entitled to do this – why should this right be denied? Others will argue that high rewards are merited – senior executives deserve to be remunerated for their expertise, experience and effort, and because of the demands of their jobs. Yet others will say that high pay for some is an inevitable feature of free market economies: gross national product is maximised in free market economies; societal welfare is maximised when GNP is maximised; therefore, high pay for the fortunate few is justified because it also indirectly benefits the many.

One of the philosophical ideas that is embedded in the standard economic world view is the principle of *desert*. This can be traced back at least to the time of Aristotle. It requires each person to be rendered benefits and burdens according to how he or she has contributed to the whole. Aristotle takes equality as a starting point, but then argues that equity (treat equals equally and unequals unequally) requires proportionality between rewards and contribution. As he says, 'this is plain from the fact that awards should be according to desert'.[40]

The principle of desert might be summarised in the following terms. Some jobs require greater levels of effort than others, are more stressful than others, or more detrimental to your health. Some jobs can only be performed by people who are appropriately qualified or have the right level of experience. It is fair that those who make a greater contribution to society, expend greater effort or incur greater personal costs should earn a higher income. Pay should reflect contribution, effort, experience and the demands of the job. This notion of distributive justice has been held for centuries and has a certain intuitive appeal. Nevertheless, it has largely gone out of fashion among modern moral philosophers, many of whom have come to see talent and ability as something of a natural lottery.

Egalitarians believe that social justice is more important than desert. They prioritise equality for all people and take it as axiomatic that all humans are equal in fundamental worth or moral status. Governments have a duty to treat each citizen under their jurisdiction with equal concern and respect. One part of this duty is the removal of economic inequalities among citizens. Our collective responsibility as citizens trumps our individual rights. A just society is characterised by equality of opportunity. No one should be disadvantaged from the start. No one should be discriminated against because of their gender, race, sexual orientation, economic background or membership in some social group. What individuals do with their opportunities is up to them. What is crucial from the standpoint of justice is that everyone's opportunities be truly equal.

The Oxford philosopher Ronald Dworkin distinguishes between the benefits and burdens that we inherit as a result of our initial position in society, and the burdens and benefits that accrue to us as a result of our own choices, actions and efforts. While it is legitimate for us to be rewarded for the second of these, it is not legitimate for us to be rewarded as a result of the first. Natural endowments of intelligence and talent are morally arbitrary and ought not to affect the distribution of resources in society.[41] This powerful defence of a broadly equalitarian view of social justice is sometimes known as 'moderate luck egalitarianism'. I shall call it *equality of opportunity*. It allows some patterned variation in the distribution of wealth in society, in contrast with more extreme forms of egalitarianism that require equality of outcomes – everyone should have the same. One of the most famous proponents of this latter view is another Oxford philosopher, G.A. Cohen, who articulated his uncompromising view in a number of books, including the aptly titled *If You're an Egalitarian, How Come You're So Rich?*[42] Cohen believes that there are very few, if any, reasons that justify large differences in the amounts that people are paid. In particular, it is difficult for well-off executives to argue with any ethical justification that they will only work hard if they are paid much better than their fellow citizens.

The *sufficientarian* view of distributive justice, sometimes associated with the American philosopher Harry Frankfurt, argues that economic equality is not, as such, of particular moral importance. When it comes to the distribution of economic goods, what matters from the point of view of morality is not that everyone should have the same but that everyone should have enough.[43] All members of society should have an income that is sufficiently high to lead a dignified life. A just society is a society in which everyone is enabled to do this. What this means will vary from society to society. Roughly speaking, to lead a dignified life is to have one's basic needs met, and to be able to meet and interact with other people as equal citizens. As long as some people do not have sufficient income to lead a decent life, it is just that income should be redistributed to them. But, once everybody has enough, no further redistribution has to take place.

Another group of scholars argue when it comes to distributive justice that property rights should take priority over desert, equality and sufficiency. The American philosopher Robert Nozick takes a libertarian perspective with his theory of *entitlement*. He contends that a person who acquires a holding of goods in a just manner, by means of a legitimate transfer, and from someone who was previously properly entitled to the goods comprised in that holding, is therefore justly entitled to those goods, even if he or she becomes inordinately wealthy as a consequence. A just society is a society in which individuals are free to engage in whatever transactions they voluntarily choose to engage in. Forced redistribution from some to others is unjust.

Entitlement theory provides ethical support for high executive pay, in particular for the type of high-powered, wealth-creating incentives that became common at the end of the 20th and beginning of the 21st centuries. According to Nozick, redistribution of income to the needy is not a matter of distributive justice but is instead a matter of charity, which he sees as distinct.

John Rawls, the philosopher encountered in the previous chapter and who was one of Robert Nozick's colleagues at Harvard, also allows for the possibility of incentives and for the differential distribution of income in society, but in a much more limited way than Nozick. Rawls recognises the legitimacy of incentives and differential levels of income if these are necessary to make the worst-off members of society as well-off as possible. He calls this 'the difference principle', although I shall call it 'maximin'. If everyone received the same amount of income no matter what choices they made, no one would be bothered to work hard. Redistributing income so as to make everyone equally well-off would therefore make everybody equally miserable. People are incentivised to work hard only if this comes with a proper reward. A just society is a society in which we tolerate the level of income inequality which is necessary to make the worst-off as well-off as they can possibly be.[44]

If we were trying to map out contemporary thinking about distributive justice, these five theories – *desert*, *equal opportunity*, *sufficiency*, *entitlement* and *maximin* – would all be important features of that map.[45] There are other theories and perspectives, and a voluminous literature on distributive justice that this short introduction cannot cover in any detail. These five theories formed the basis of our empirical study, which I will describe in a moment.

To these we added a sixth principle – a less well-known idea that we derived from the business ethics literature and which sits neatly between the economic and philosophical ideas about high pay. This is known as the 'market failures approach' to business ethics, which is most closely associated with the Canadian philosopher Joseph Heath. Heath argues that the rationale for shareholder value maximisation is to establish competition among firms. Competition drives prices toward market-clearing levels, benefitting consumers, and delivering for society an efficient allocation of resources and labour. The function of the market economy is to produce the most efficient use of resources possible.

Economists have demonstrated that allocative efficiency requires competitive markets. They have also demonstrated that monopolies, market failures and negative externalities (costs to third parties, like pollution, that are not captured by the price mechanism) interfere with the efficient operation of markets, and undermine allocative efficiency. They argue that market prices in themselves are neither just nor unjust. Under ideal conditions, market prices carry information about the relative scarcity of resources, thereby allowing us to allocate resources to where they can be put to their most valuable use. It is misguided to think that there is such a thing as a 'just wage'.

The market failures approach to business ethics argues that a robust moral code can be developed on the back of free market economics. If perfect competition produces the best outcome for society, then actions that deliberately depart from perfect competition are unethical. Income is the price paid for labour. We have an ethical responsibility to see to it that wages are free from distortions, so that they carry information about relative scarcity. An ethical manager is one who seeks to maximise the firm's profits while operating both within the terms of the law and also in the spirit of perfect competition – thus cognisant of the problems of monopolies, market failures and externalities. An ethical businessperson should seek to create the conditions necessary for private enterprises to produce an efficient allocation of goods and services in the economy.

I shall call the principle behind the market failures approach 'efficiency', for reasons that I hope are self-evident. Interestingly, the market failures approach is consistent with the thinking of the medieval philosophers, who believed that there is such a thing as a 'just wage'. As has already been explained, this was linked to the medieval concept of social hierarchy, and corresponded to a reasonable charge that would enable someone to live and support their family on a scale suitable to their station in life, as well as to reproduce skills in their offspring. According to many scholars of the time, the just price did not correspond to costs – as determined, for example, by social status – but was simply the current market price, though with an important reservation: in a case of usury, of collusion, or where the price could not easily be determined by the market, public authorities retained the right to interfere and to impose a fair wage.[46]

Perhaps counter-intuitively, the efficiency principle does not necessarily provide justification for high pay. I have already suggested that high executive pay might be a result of a labour market failure – perhaps senior executives are paid more than is necessary to command their services, and are receiving economic rents – payments in excess of what might truly be the hypothetical market clearing wage. In this case the market failures approach would regard very high pay as unethical and in need of fixing.

Social comparisons

In 1966 the sociologist W.G. Runciman asked the question 'how does social order persist in the face of widespread social inequality?' He concluded that, when it comes to comparisons of incomes, we are only interested in a narrowly defined reference group – we care about how those close to us are doing much more than those in very different social situations. We do not see the world in terms of the abstract categories favoured by sociologists or philosophers but focus instead on comparing ourselves with family, friends and workmates.[47] Runciman's highly influential findings continue to be the received wisdom among sociologists, although the empirical research on which it is based now took place over 50 years ago.

How can this be? Why is it that people appear to be interested in micro-level social comparisons, where small differences can take on great significance, while at the same time generally discounting macro-level distributive justice? It may be because people do not care what those in very different social situations actually earn. It may be because they are resigned to their position, knowing that there is little or nothing they can do about any disparity, however unfair they think it is. Or it may be simply because they do not have enough information about other people's earnings. To illustrate this last point, in 1999 the British Social Attitudes Survey, which asks a random sample of around 3,000 people what it is like to live in Britain and what they think about how the country is run, included questions about the perceptions of gross annual earnings for different occupations, one being 'chairman of a large corporation'. The general perception at the time was that such an individual probably earned around £125,000 (equivalent to £220,000 in 2020 terms), that they should really earn, in a normative sense, about £75,000 (£130,000 in 2020 terms), and yet the actual reported earnings of someone in this occupational category at the time was on average around £555,000 (just under £1 million in 2020).[48]

It is hard to know to what extent social reference theory, as it is known, still applies when it comes to public attitudes to top pay. Certainly today, because of changes in disclosure requirements about directors' pay in the US, UK and many other countries, much more is known about top pay than it was in the past. Reports of egregiously high CEO pay now seem to appear regularly in the press, particularly when some acute disparity – like companies declining to make up 80 per cent furlough payments to employees during the COVID–19 pandemic while at the same time paying bonuses to top executives – brings matters into sharp relief.[49]

In the 2020 British Social Attitudes Survey, 77 per cent of people answered 'unfair' or 'very unfair' to the question 'how fair or unfair do you think income distribution is in Britain?', suggesting that macro-level distributive justice is an issue that companies and investors should take seriously.[50]

To sum up

In this chapter I have described three main economic theories about executive pay, provided a short introduction to distributive justice, and explained six different principles of justice advocated by different philosophers. These principles include desert (the idea that certain people deserve to receive economic advantages because of superior contribution, effort or experience, or because of the specific demands of the job), sufficiency (the belief that all members of society are entitled to a level of income that is sufficiently high for them to lead a dignified life), the difference principle (or maximin, the idea that differential rewards are justified if and only if they enable the worst-off to be as well-off as possible), moderate luck egalitarianism (equality of opportunity while holding people responsible for their own choices), entitlement theory (people are entitled to transfer their holdings to whomsoever they desire, so that acquired property rights trump all other theories about distributive justice), and efficiency (the idea that a just distribution of income is one that leads to an efficient allocation of labour and other resources).[51]

CHAPTER 3

What do business executives think about distributive justice?

In this chapter I introduce an empirical study of what business executives think about distributive justice, drawing upon the views of over one thousand senior executives from around the world. These data were obtained using a survey instrument that was based on a philosophical thought experiment resembling John Rawls's original position, which I explain in more detail below. I show how what business executives think about distributive justice resolves into four clusters: 'welfare liberals' 'egalitarians', 'meritocrats' and 'free marketeers'. In subsequent chapters I will examine these groups in turn, drawing on the ideas of various representative moral philosophers.

How to cite this book chapter:
Pepper, A. 2022. *If You're So Ethical, Why Are You So Highly Paid?: Ethics, Inequality and Executive Pay.* London: LSE Press. Pp. 39–48.
DOI: https://doi.org/10.31389/lsepress/eth License: CC BY-NC

Empirical study

In order to make this study an empirical and not merely a theoretical exercise, working with two academic colleagues, Dr Susanne Burri, a moral philosopher, and Dr Daniela Lup, who helped with the statistical analysis, and with the support of PwC, we carried out a philosophical thought experiment with 1,123 participants from around the world to test what people working in high-status jobs think about distributive justice. We used a market research agency to gather data about ethical preferences using a questionnaire that we designed. Participants were encouraged to think of themselves as in Rawls's 'original position' when answering the questions. The preamble to the questionnaire described the following situation:

> Suppose that from tomorrow onwards, you find yourself in an imaginary society where the skills and talents that are relevant to economic prosperity are very different from the ones that you are currently familiar with. In this society you might, for example, have a successful career if you are prepared to perform monotonous tasks for hours at a time, or if you are able to carry heavy objects over large distances. Other skills and knowledge may also be rewarded in this imaginary society – or they may not be – the point is that you don't know when making your decisions.

We primed the participants with a general question: 'what principles governing the distribution of income would you want to apply in the society in which you lived if you did not know your place in that society?' The questionnaire addressed the six different principles of distributive justice described in the previous chapter: desert, equal opportunity, sufficiency, entitlement, maximin and efficiency. These are summarised in Figure 3.1.

Figure 3.1: Six principles of distributive justice

Principle	Description
Desert	Some people deserve to receive certain economic advantages in light of their contribution, effort, experience, and the demands of the job.
Equal opportunity	Everyone ought to have the same non-discriminatory access to positions and posts that come with economic advantages.
Sufficiency	All members of a society should have an income that is sufficiently high to lead a dignified life.
Entitlement	Whatever income someone voluntarily pays to someone else is just.
Maximin	Income should be distributed so as to make the worst-off members of a society as well-off as possible.
Efficiency	The right distribution of income is that which leads to an efficient allocation of labour.

In respect of each of the six principles, participants in the study were invited to comment on whether they would want to live in an imaginary society in which they found themselves to be governed by the principle, whether a society governed by the principle would be a just society, and whether they thought that the society they currently live in was actually governed by the principle. The questions were then repeated in terms of the application of distributive justice to a hypothetical large global corporation in which they might work, so that we had data at two levels of analysis, at both society and company level.[52] We gathered data from senior executives, with titles such as chairman, CEO, president, senior vice president and so on. The resulting sample comprised over one thousand participants from around the world. Two-thirds of participants were male and one-third female. Incomes ranged from US$150,000 to over US$1,000,000. Over 30 countries and more than 25 industry groups were represented in the sample. Approximately 50 per cent of the employing companies were public corporations, 40 per cent were private companies and 10 per cent were state-owned enterprises. For anyone who is interested in the details, I have provided more information about the sample and results in the Appendix.

It was evident from our survey that executives appeared to take distributive justice very seriously. They engaged with the process, some telling us about the amount of time that they had taken to digest the questions and reflect on their answers. They agreed or strongly agreed with more principles of justice than they disavowed. The narrative comments that many of them provided were consistent with a serious ethical perspective on pay and inequality.

Our first most striking observation was the pronounced degree of pluralism. Participants indicated that they believed in the truth of a number of different principles of distributive justice. Over 90 per cent of respondents agreed with more than one justice principle, and more than 50 per cent subscribed to four or more principles. Pluralism increased with seniority but was otherwise relatively homogenous across demographic factors such as gender, nationality, industry sector and type of company.

Many philosophers who have written about justice, from Plato onwards, have assumed that there is one, and only one, distributive system that philosophy can properly endorse. Others argue that pluralism is nothing to be afraid of. The prominent American political theorist Michael Walzer, in an influential book entitled *Spheres of Justice – A Defense of Pluralism and Equality*, argues that no 'single distributive criterion … can possibly match the diversity of social goods'.[53] He argues instead for a sophisticated pluralistic theory of justice. In much the same way, David Miller argues that principles of justice 'must be understood contextually', depending upon 'different forms of human association and reflecting the complexity of modern society'.[54] In the textbook on ethics which he co-authored with James Tufts, John Dewey put it like this:

> A genuinely reflective morals will look upon all codes as possible data; it will consider the conditions under which they arose; the methods which consciously or unconsciously determine their formation and acceptance; it will inquire into their applicability in present conditions. It will neither insist dogmatically upon some of them, nor idly throw them all away of no significance. It will treat them as a storehouse of information and possible indications of what is now right and good.[55]

Four clusters

Norms of distributive justice are typically viewed by social commentators (although not necessarily by philosophers) as a continuum, with 'equality' or 'community' at one end and 'free entitlement' or 'individuality' at the other end.[56] I prefer to conceptualise distributive justice as a 'field', a bit like a force field in physics.[57] Imagine, if you can, a six-dimensional space with the six principles of distributive justice each forming a separate axis or dimension. By performing what statisticians call a cluster analysis we were able to observe four distinct participant–particle groups (or 'clusters') in what is in mathematical terms a six-dimensional space. Two of these clusters, which we call 'relational egalitarians' and 'welfare liberals', focused on the community, endorsing merit-based principles to some extent, but only in combination with a sufficientarian floor constraint. For relational egalitarians, needs and equal opportunities trumped other things and were clearly more important than talent, effort and contribution. The welfare liberals to some extent shared John Rawls's belief that rewards for contribution are desirable as long as the benefits spill over to others: the populist economic principle of 'a rising tide raises all boats'. However, neither of these two clusters saw any role for the principle of entitlement. The 'meritocrats', as we call them, were concerned with rewarding productivity, which they combined with a strong focus on equal opportunities and sufficiency. Their thought seemed to be that, while we should try to reward differential contributions differentially, we also have demanding duties of justice towards our society's most disadvantaged members. Finally, 'free marketeers' focused more on individuals' rights. They rejected needs-based principles, instead conceptualising distributive justice as based entirely upon merit and efficiency. As they saw it, distributive justice is about rewarding talent and ensuring that a functioning price mechanism leads to an efficient allocation of resources. Descriptions of these four clusters – relational egalitarians, welfare liberals, meritocrats and free marketeers – are set out in Figure 3.2.

It is of course hard to imagine (and impossible to picture) a six-dimensional space, even if it can be conceptualised mathematically. While Figure 3.3 is a second-best and somewhat imperfect representation, you might find it easier to imagine the four clusters in a two-dimensional hexagonal plane cutting across the six-dimensional space. You can picture an individual-focus section at the north-west end of the plane and a community-focus section at the south-east. Free marketeers would be located in the north-west section, where they would be most closely associated with 'desert' and 'efficiency'. Free marketeers believe in the inherent justice of free markets which provide individuals with the rewards they deserve because of the contribution they make

Figure 3.2: Four clusters of respondents' attitudes

Cluster	Characteristics
Relational egalitarians	All members of a community should have an income that is sufficient for them to lead a dignified life. Equal opportunities are important – nobody should be at a disadvantage because of the circumstances of their birth or because of brute bad luck. There is no automatic entitlement to income or wealth. Talent, effort and contribution are not the main criteria for allocating economic benefits.
Welfare liberals	People should be rewarded for the contribution that they make to their communities, principally with a view to making the worst-off as well-off as possible. All members of a community should have an income that is sufficient for them to lead a dignified life. There is no automatic entitlement to income or wealth. Efficiency is not the only criterion by which outcomes should be judged.
Meritocrats	Some people deserve to receive economic benefits because of their efforts or the demands of the job. Equal opportunities are important – nobody should be at a disadvantage because of the circumstances of their birth or because of brute bad luck. There is no automatic entitlement to income or wealth. The well-off do not have an automatic obligation to support the worst-off. Efficiency is not the only criterion by which outcomes should be judged.
Free marketeers	Talented people deserve to receive economic benefits. Everyone should have the opportunity to demonstrate their ability. Efficiency is the main criterion for determining how income should be allocated. No one is automatically entitled to income or wealth. The well-off do not have an automatic obligation to support the worst-off.

to value creation. Welfare liberals would be located in the south and relational egalitarians at the south-east end of the plane. Welfare liberals are community-minded people who believe in

Figure 3.3: How the four clusters draw on the six principles

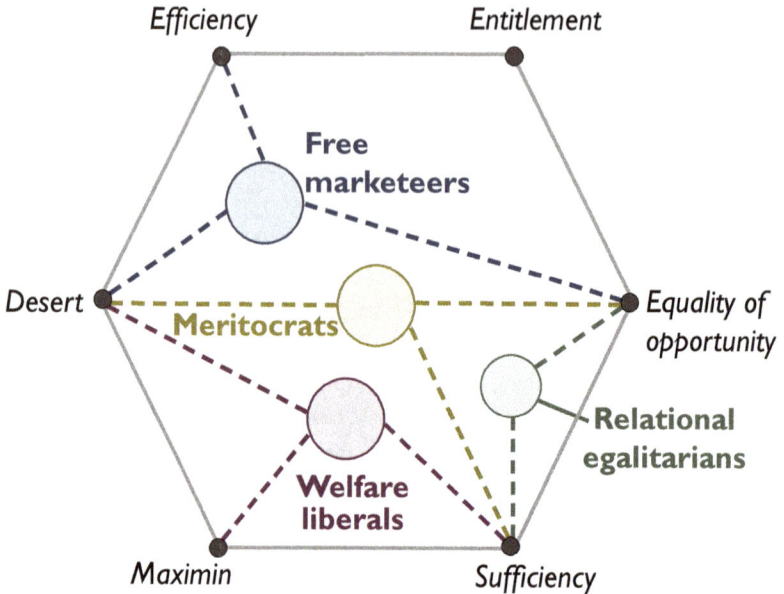

the importance of sufficiency and equal opportunity, but critically they also recognise the importance of Rawlsian incentives if the worst-off are to be made as well-off as possible. Relational egalitarians are first and foremost welfare-minded and accept the principle that all members of a community should have an income that is sufficiently high to lead a dignified life as a priority. Meritocrats, located somewhere in the middle of the hexagonal plane, recognise the importance of sufficiency and equal opportunities, but nevertheless believe that individuals deserve to receive economic benefits because of their efforts or the demands of their jobs. The dotted lines tie each of the four clusters to their dominant principles of justice.

An analogy with reference to the English secondary school system may help to locate these clusters somewhere in your minds. Relational egalitarians would probably support a comprehensive school system, in which state schools are open to all and do not select on the basis of academic achievement or aptitude. Welfare liberals would prefer selective schooling but would be happy if this took place within a comprehensive school setting. Meritocrats would support state grammar schools for the most able. Free marketeers would want parents to be able to pay for the education of their children, but might baulk at the most expensive schools, which buy hard-to-justify benefits for the most privileged.

Three of the four clusters in our sample (welfare liberals, meritocrats and free marketeers) were of broadly equivalent size with around 300 members. The relational egalitarian cluster was slightly smaller, with just under 200 members.[58] (Full results are detailed in the Appendix; see Figure A.5.) While some variations in views about distributive justice across the four clusters were apparent in the data, there were few significant differences in terms of age, gender, income, nationality, company type or industry sector. This is consistent with other published empirical studies, which report that views on distributive justice do not differ significantly between socio-economic classes and different cultures.[59] Having said this, we did find a small number of important differences between clusters. I will comment on these and other characteristics of the four clusters in the following chapters as I continue to tell the story of distributive justice and how it applies to high pay.

To sum up

In this chapter I have described how we went about collecting the thoughts of senior executives about the six principles of distributive justice – desert, equal opportunity, sufficiency, entitlement, maximin and efficiency – using a questionnaire in which we asked the participants to imagine themselves in a Rawlsian 'original position' from which to make considered judgements about justice. I have explained how the results of the survey coalesced around four distinct clusters, to which I now turn. I begin, for reasons that I will explain, with welfare liberals.

CHAPTER 4

Welfare liberals

Welfare liberals believe that people should be rewarded for the contribution they make to their communities, informed by a belief that this will help to make the worst-off as well-off as possible. They argue that this must be underpinned by a safety net, which guarantees that all members of a community have an income that is sufficient for them to lead a dignified life. This group of executives responding to the survey said things like:

- 'I agree with the principle that guarantees the welfare of all society without exception, always thinking about the dignity of all people, including the most disadvantaged, but also recognising the importance of freedom of choice, equal opportunities, and encouraging talent – we need both.'

How to cite this book chapter:
Pepper, A. 2022. *If You're So Ethical, Why Are You So Highly Paid?: Ethics, Inequality and Executive Pay.* London: LSE Press. Pp. 49–55.
DOI: https://doi.org/10.31389/lsepress/eth License: CC BY-NC

- 'Those who have more must contribute more to society.'
- 'There must always be the principle of collective responsibility for those who have less – we must act with social responsibility towards our neighbour who suffers a greater degree of poverty, under the principle of "love for your neighbour".'

Welfare liberals cluster at the conjunction of three principles of distributive justice: maximin – most closely associated with John Rawls, who we met in Chapter 1 – sufficiency and desert. I deal with maximin and sufficiency in this chapter. Desert is most closely associated with meritocrats and will be covered in Chapter 6. I begin with Rawls.

John Rawls

John Rawls is widely regarded as one of the leading moral and political philosophers of the modern age. As a college student in the US at the start of the Second World War, Rawls first considered training for the priesthood, but eventually chose philosophy over theology, and became a career academic. He studied at Princeton under Norman Malcolm, a disciple of Ludwig Wittgenstein, and then at Oxford, where he worked with Isaiah Berlin and Stuart Hampshire. In this way he had a rigorous training in analytical philosophy. Rawls eventually settled at Harvard, where he taught for over 30 years.[60] A *Theory of Justice*, his most famous work, was first published in 1971. It is generally regarded even by its critics as the most important work of moral and political philosophy of the 20th century.[61] Rawls proposes that the correct principles of justice can be derived by imagining what rules would be agreed by free and rational persons standing behind a 'veil of ignorance' in which they did not know their class, race, sex, intelligence or general ability, in an imagined 'original position'. He argues that, in these circumstances, rational persons would, at a minimum, insist on the following two principles. First, each person is to have an equal right to the most extensive scheme of equal basic liberties compatible with a similar scheme of liberties for others. Second, social and economic inequalities are to be arranged so that they are both reasonably expected to be to everyone's advantage, and attached to positions and offices open to all. The first of these principles, Rawls says, takes 'lexical priority' over the second – basic liberties must be ensured before turning attention to social and economic inequalities; you cannot trade basic liberties for greater social and economic equality.[62]

The first principle Rawls calls 'the principle of greatest equal liberty', sometimes shortened to 'the freedom principle'. Rawls regards this as paramount. The second comes in two parts: 'the principle of fair equality of opportunity' and 'the difference principle'. From these principles, which he takes as more or less axiomatic, Rawls derives a framework of rules and further principles of justice to regulate the distribution of all social and economic goods. The primary social goods, to give them broad categories, are rights, liberties and opportunities. The primary economic goods are income and wealth. You will notice that Rawls defines 'goods' more broadly than the definition of economic goods that I provided in Chapter 1.

The distribution of income and wealth is primarily determined by the difference principle, which Rawls explains as follows. Consider the distribution of economic goods among social groups. Imagine that the distribution of income and wealth varies between, at one end of the spectrum, an entrepreneurial or property-owning group and, at the other end of the spectrum, a group of unskilled workers. What can justify the unequal distribution of income and wealth between these two groups? According to the difference principle, an unequal distribution of goods 'is justifiable only if the difference in expectation is to the advantage of the representative man who is worse off, in this case the representative unskilled worker'.[63] In other words, a just distribution system is one that maximises the incomes of the least well-off.

The difference principle provides a solution to a problem that arises in welfare economics because of its definition of Pareto efficiency. The Pareto criterion (that an outcome is efficient if no one can be bettered without making somebody else worse off) considers all efficiency improvements equally desirable – differentiating between them involves making value judgements. The difference principle allows for the ranking of Pareto efficient outcomes – the Pareto improvement, which betters the lot of the worst-off member of society by the most is the one most preferred.[64]

Some people will regard it as self-evident that differential rewards are justified by differences in effort and talent – that some people deserve to be paid more than others. Surely it is legitimate, they say, to pay top managers more than shop floor workers because of their greater ability, education and experience. Similarly, might it not be argued that shareholders, who provide passive financial capital, should be rewarded less highly, pro rata to their units of invested capital, than top managers, who provide active human capital, given the amount of effort respectively invested?

Welfare liberals are somewhat sympathetic to such desert claims, and desert (which I will examine in more detail in Chapter 6) is certainly a factor in their thinking. But for welfare liberals desert is moderated by the difference principle, which only provides the ethical justification for low-powered, muted or, as the economist John Roberts calls them, 'weak' incentives.[65] Differential pay is necessary to ensure that all are adequately incentivised to perform at their best for the good of society as a whole, but high-powered, inequality-generating incentives would undermine societal cohesion and hence are not to be encouraged. Welfare liberals are more focused on ensuring that the worst-off members of society, the 'representative unskilled workers', are paid a sufficient amount to ensure that their basic needs are met.

Sufficientarianism

The origins of modern thinking about sufficiency can probably be traced back to an influential article by the American philosopher Harry Frankfurt. Frankfurt, formerly professor of philosophy at Princeton, is famous for his 'no nonsense' approach to philosophical reasoning, preferring brevity and non-technical language. His 1986 paper 'On Bullshit' was reissued as a book in 2005 and became a surprise bestseller. In it he says that what we might now call 'fake news' is not lying as it has no regard for the truth. He argues that 'it is impossible for someone to lie unless he knows the truth. Producing bullshit requires no such conviction'.[66] In another paper, which was reissued as a book called *On Inequality*, Frankfurt takes aim at economic egalitarianism, the idea that it is desirable for everyone to have the same amount of money. Much of the book is taken up with arguments intended to disabuse the reader of the merits of egalitarianism, which Frankfurt regards as being of no particular moral consequence. While doing so he sets out an alternative ethical principle:

> Economic equality is not, as such, of particular moral importance. With respect to the distribution of economic assets what *is* important from the point of view of morality is not that everyone should have the *same* but that everyone should have *enough*. If everyone had enough,

> it would be of no moral consequence whether some had
> more than others. I shall refer to this … as 'the doctrine
> of sufficiency'.[67]

Frankfurt argues that we are morally obliged to eliminate poverty, not to reduce or eliminate inequality. The poor suffer because they do not have enough, not because others have more or because some appear to have too much. The focus should be on ensuring that everyone has a sufficient amount to lead a dignified life. To focus instead on eliminating inequality is to miss this fundamental point. Ensuring that everyone has enough may help to reduce inequality, but that is merely a side effect. To focus on reducing inequality by heavily taxing the rich, a policy of many postwar left-wing governments, does not necessarily help to solve the problems of the poor. The goal of political policies aimed at achieving social justice should be to end poverty, not inequality.

But Frankfurt is not an apologist for inequality – he is a liberal rather than a libertarian. He argues that the conjunction of vast wealth and extreme poverty is morally offensive and believes that the beneficiaries of vast wealth should reflect on this. However, focusing on high pay without considering the effects of redistribution on the objective of eliminating poverty is not particularly helpful. Inequality in itself, according to Frankfurt, has no intrinsic moral significance. Better a society where everyone has enough, even if some have far more, than a society where differentials are smaller but some people struggle financially.

To sum up

Welfare liberals believe in the power of free markets, but would choose an efficient outcome that maximises the lot of the worst-off members of society over any other. They also believe that a community or society safety net is necessary, so that everyone has an income that is sufficient to lead a dignified life. Merit is important when allocating resources, but not as much as the general welfare. These are not, according to welfare liberals, merely societal issues; they are also matters for companies to consider. Employers have a responsibility to pay a living wage. Their activities should be focused on improving the welfare of the whole of society, including, most importantly, the worst-off.

CHAPTER 5

Relational egalitarians

Relational egalitarians believe most importantly that all members of a community should have an income that is sufficient for them to lead a dignified life. Equal opportunities are also important – nobody should be at a disadvantage because of the circumstances of their birth or because of brute bad luck. On the other hand, nobody has an automatic entitlement to income or wealth; nor are talent, effort and personal contribution the main criteria for allocating economic benefits. This group gave responses such as:

- 'Everyone should have the same benefits and same opportunities – people should have the same educational opportunities that allow them to access jobs with fair payments according to their abilities and desires.'
- 'A society in which wealth inflation can be greater than savings potential on minimum wages will never be just

How to cite this book chapter:
Pepper, A. 2022. *If You're So Ethical, Why Are You So Highly Paid?: Ethics, Inequality and Executive Pay.* London: LSE Press. Pp. 57–66.
DOI: https://doi.org/10.31389/lsepress/eth License: CC BY-NC

> – we need a method that can address this, which makes property and wealth accumulation more accessible objectives for all.'

- 'Markets do not work – either in terms of labour or trade – skills in high demand are more easily developed or bought through high cost education or work experience by those with existing wealth or social status.'

I have already discussed 'sufficientarianism' in the previous chapter. Sufficientarians believe that the most important principle of distributive justice is that all members of society should have an income that is sufficiently high to lead a dignified life. When it comes to how income is shared in society, this, they believe, takes priority over everything else. However, unlike Harry Frankfurt, who believed that economic equality was not, as such, of particular moral importance, relational egalitarians combine a belief in the importance of sufficiency with a focus on equality of opportunity. In this chapter I will examine the ideas of two leading egalitarians, G.A. Cohen and Ronald Dworkin.

The dispute between John Rawls and G.A. Cohen

Gerald Allan Cohen, better known as G.A. Cohen or Jerry Cohen, was a Canadian philosopher who for many years held the position of Chichele Professor of Social and Political Theory at All Souls College, Oxford. Cohen was one of a number of scholars known as 'analytical Marxists', who used the techniques of analytical philosophy along with tools of modern social science such as rational choice theory to help elucidate the ideas of Karl Marx. Cohen called this 'non-bullshit Marxism'. He later became known for his work on distributive justice, especially egalitarianism, which he expounded in two books, *If You're an Egalitarian, How Come You're So Rich?* (2000) and *Rescuing Justice and Equality* (2008).

Cohen exposes what he believes to be certain weaknesses in Rawls's theory. He begins by identifying the underlying paradox in Rawls's argument when he says that 'the difference principle can be used to justify paying incentives that induce inequalities only when the attitude of talented people runs counter to the spirit of the difference principle.'[68] This means that, while it may be 'intelligent policy', the difference principle is not, according to Cohen, a principle of 'justice'.

To illustrate this point, Cohen quotes an exchange between two individuals, 'Well-off' and 'Worse-off', imagined by the Canadian philosopher Jan Narveson:

Well-off:	'Look here, fellow citizen, I'll work hard and make both you and me better off, provided I get a bigger share than you.'
Worse-off:	'Well that's rather good; but I thought you were agreeing that justice requires equality?'
Well-off:	'Yes, but that's only a benchmark, you see. To do still better, both of us, you understand, may require differential incentive payments to people like me.'
Worse-off:	'Oh. Well, what makes them necessary?'
Well-off:	'What makes them necessary is that I won't work as hard if I don't get more than you.'
Worse-off:	Well, why not?'
Well-off:	'I dunno... I guess that's just the way I'm built.'[69]

Cohen identifies a series of ambiguities in Rawls's theory. Is the difference principle permissive or mandatory? Does it merely require committing no harm or does it entail actually helping? Does it, to use the language of agency theory, apply to both

Figure 5.1: Cohen's analysis of the difference principle

	Mandated	Permitted
Helping actions are…	(a)	(b)
Non-harming actions are…	(c)	(d)

'principals' and 'agents' in the same way? Does the difference principle matter equally in existing societal structures that are inherently unequal, or just in the original position, where there are no recognised inequalities? Should it only be considered a principle of justice at society level, or is it also an ethical principle for individuals?[70] We might add: is the difference principle part of the ethical framework that should be adopted by companies?

The first two ambiguities can be considered together. Cohen points out that there is initial uncertainty about the difference principle along two dimensions: does Rawls require the more fortunate to help the less fortunate, or merely to commit no harm; and, a related consideration, is action by the more fortunate mandated or merely permitted? He represents these options in a matrix set out in Figure 5.1.

A number of logical positions can be inferred from this matrix, of which the most obvious are, first, the weak form of the difference principle, a combination of (b) and (c), whereby helping actions are permitted and non-harming actions mandated (that is, decisions that harm the less fortunate are prohibited), and, second, the strong form of the difference principle, that is, (a), whereby helping actions are mandated in all circumstances.

Buried in here is another point, which I shall call 'the standpoint argument': to what extent does the difference principle place obligations on well-off agents as opposed to principals or neutral observers? Imagine the following situation: a CEO says to the chair of the remuneration committee, 'I am not adequately incentivised; unless you pay me more, I will either withhold effort or find a job elsewhere.' The remuneration committee chair reasons as follows. 'The CEO has unique skills that would be extremely difficult to replace. If he leaves this will be to the detriment of the company, its shareholders and its employees, including low-paid employees. It is in the interests of all these stakeholders that the services of the CEO should be retained, even at greater cost. Therefore, I must accede to his request.' Cohen points out that, while this line of thinking is entirely reasonable and, hence, arguably, ethical from the standpoint of the remuneration committee chair, the CEO's personal position is tantamount to blackmail, and is therefore not ethical in any sense of the word. You may recognise this as an instance of the remuneration committee's dilemma, which we met in Chapter 2.

Cohen also draws attention to the importance of the starting position. His other criticism of Rawls is another version of what he calls 'standpoint' but I shall call 'level of analysis', to distinguish it from one of my previous arguments. Rawls argues that distributive justice is a matter for the state to deal with, to be addressed, for example, by taxation. Rawlsians have resisted the temptation to extend the difference principle to individuals or corporate persons. The state's task is to set out a just institutional framework. The individual's and corporation's task is to operate as best they can within that framework. This is a further example of Rawls being analytically minimalist, by which I mean that the whole edifice of his theory of justice is designed to make as few appeals as logically possible to naturalistic principles or intuition – that indeed is one of its strengths, to treat as little as possible as self-evident or to be taken for granted. Cohen challenges this, arguing as follows.

There is, first, the Rawlsian view that distributive justice is a task for the state alone. A second view would say that the individual must show some regard to what the state is fully dedicated to in this domain. Finally, there is my own view, which is that both the state, with no life of its own, and the individual, who is indeed thus endowed, must, in appropriate different fashions, show regard in economic matters both to impersonal justice and to the legitimate demands of the individual. … [T]he individual who affirms the difference principle must have some regard to it in his economic choices, whatever regard, that is, which starts where his personal prerogative stops.[71]

In other words, Cohen is not prepared to let individuals off the hook when it comes to questions about distributive justice. If they believe that a principle is applicable at societal level, then they should be prepared to internalise that principle and make it part of their own personal ethical value set. This is, Cohen would say, as true for the CEO as it is for the state and the remuneration committee chair.

Ronald Dworkin

Ronald Dworkin was, like G.A. Cohen, a North American who found a long-term home at Oxford, but in other respects the two were very different. Dworkin studied philosophy at Harvard before turning to law at Oxford and Harvard Law School. After clerking for Judge Learned Hand of the United States Court of Appeals (what a wonderful personal name, incidentally, for a member of the judiciary!), working as an attorney for New York City law firm Sullivan and Cromwell, and teaching law at Yale and New York University law schools, Dworkin was appointed in 1969 to the Chair of Jurisprudence at Oxford, where he remained until

1998. Dworkin was a straight-A student, known for his intellectual brilliance and formidable capacity for work.

Dworkin believed that law was underpinned by the moral principles of justice and fairness. Like Cohen, he was an egalitarian. His theory of distributive justice is set out in two seminal articles, both entitled 'What Is Equality?', as well as a book, *Sovereign Virtue*, in which he addresses what has sometimes been called the 'equality of what' question and advances his theory of 'equality of resources'.[72] Dworkin takes as a starting point for his ethical theory the principle that citizens should be treated equally unless there are good reasons for treating them differently. That is, he says, part of the covenant that society makes with its members. He then poses the important question 'equality of what?' and lists a number of possibilities, before alighting upon two things in particular, which he calls 'welfare' and 'resources'. He brings these two concepts to life by describing the following imaginary scenario.

> Suppose, for example, that a man of some wealth has several children, one of whom is blind, another a playboy with expensive tastes, a third a prospective politician with expensive ambitions, another a poet with humble needs, another a sculptor who works in expensive material, and so on. How shall he draw his will? If he takes equality of welfare as his goal, then he will take these differences among his children into account, so that he will not leave them equal shares. Of course he will have to decide on some interpretation of welfare and whether, for example, expensive tastes should figure in his calculations in the same way as handicaps or expensive ambitions. But if, on the contrary, he takes equality of resources as his goal then, assuming his children have roughly equal wealth already, he may well decide that his goal requires an equal division of his wealth.[73]

Dworkin proceeds, in the first of his two articles, to explain why equality of welfare will not do. He points out that welfarism, in its modern conception, focuses on the satisfaction of personal preferences, and identifies a series of problems with this. He argues that preferences are inherently subjective, that tastes (for example, for the good life) and needs (such as for a basic level of sustenance) may constitute preferences of equal strength to different persons, but that this does not give them equivalent ethical status. He comments on the perennial problem of inter-personal comparisons of different people's preferences (how do we know that your preference for X is in any way comparable to my preference for Y) and the general problems that exist with preference measurement. He asks whether ethical welfarism should be based on the preferences that we do have or the preferences that we *should* have? He concludes by proposing that 'resources', the subject of his second article, are a much more objective measure than welfare.

Dworkin continues, in his second article, to explain why equality of resources is a better answer to the question 'equality of what', what he means by 'resources' in this context, and how equality of resources might come about. Like Rawls and Nozick before him, he uses a thought experiment to develop his theory. He describes a second scenario. A group of sailors is shipwrecked on a desert island with no realistic hope of rescue. The island has abundant resources and no native population. The sailors accept the principle that no one has an automatic right to any of the island's resources, and agree that a fair way must be found of dividing the resources among themselves. They also accept a principle that they call the 'envy test', that no division of resources will be regarded as fair if, after the division, any person would prefer another person's bundle of resources.[74] To facilitate the process of division they establish a counting mechanism that enables relative values to be placed on different kinds of resources. They appoint one of the sailors, who has a reputation for fairness and good judgement, as an independent adjudicator, to divide up the island's resources into bundles. Through the process of initial allocation by the independent adjudicator, and subsequent exchange through an open and fair market mechanism, they arrive at an equal division of bundles of resources that everyone is happy with.

So far so good: we appear to have achieved an equitable division of resources. However, Dworkin points out two problems in particular. First, it is likely that the sailors will arrive on the island with antecedent advantages and disadvantages. Some may have skills and abilities that make them particularly suited to island life, while others may be handicapped in some way. Second, while the initial division of resources may be demonstrably fair (ignoring for the moment the antecedent capabilities and handicaps of the recipients), over time the situation will change. Some sailors will make bad decisions about how to use their resources. Others will experience bad luck that they could not have anticipated, such as natural disasters. Dworkin calls the first 'option luck', a matter of how deliberate and calculated gambles turn out, and the second 'brute luck', how risks fall out that are in no sense deliberate gambles consciously taken by responsible decision-makers.

Dworkin believe that justice requires antecedent differences and brute luck to be equalised, whereas differential effort (for example, in the case of the sailor who succeeds by working hard and putting his resources to good use) and option luck (the result of wise decision-making about the way that initial resources are put to use) do not need to be equalised. For this reason he is sometimes described as a 'luck egalitarian' (although he does not necessarily accept the title): a just society is characterised by equal access to resources that come with economic benefits; no one should be disadvantaged from the start because of the circumstances in which they find themselves through no fault of their own; no one should be discriminated against because of the circumstances of their birth; and what individuals do with their opportunities is up to them – what is crucial from the standpoint of justice is that people are not disadvantaged because of brute bad luck.[75]

To sum up

The relational egalitarians are the smallest of the four clusters in our original survey of business executives but still a group of significant size. They believe, far more than the other three clusters, that fairness trumps merit when it comes to determining how income should be allocated. It is only fair that everyone has the same opportunities and benefits, educational and otherwise, in order to allow equal access to the job market and to job opportunities. Companies have a responsibility to pay a living wage, to ensure that everyone has enough to lead a dignified life. All this is not just a matter for the state – companies too have responsibilities to help ensure that there is social justice.

CHAPTER 6

Meritocrats

Meritocrats believe that justice in pay is primarily a matter of desert. They argue that some people deserve to receive economic benefits because of their efforts or the demands of the job. But they also believe that equal opportunities are important – nobody should be at a disadvantage because of the circumstances of their birth or because of brute bad luck. They said:

- 'In a society which values contribution, effort, skill and experience, the major focus should be on impact and contribution.'
- 'All people should have opportunities in the job market equally, but their appointment should depend solely on their effort and not on external influences. … People should only be promoted on merit.'

How to cite this book chapter:
Pepper, A. 2022. *If You're So Ethical, Why Are You So Highly Paid?: Ethics, Inequality and Executive Pay.* London: LSE Press. Pp. 67–79.
DOI: https://doi.org/10.31389/lsepress/eth License: CC BY-NC

- 'Ideally remuneration should be based on merit (qualifications, special ability, skill shortage, special responsibility, commitment, entrepreneurial spirit, and so on). ... People who simply do not make an effort should also only receive the absolute subsistence level of support.'

Desert

One of the shibboleths of modern management theory is 'thou shalt link pay to performance'.[76] To a manager or management scholar, the idea that pay and reward should be based on performance or merit or, as philosophers prefer to call it, desert (on what is deserved) seems blindingly obvious (although the devil is in the details, especially as regards the time period over which performance is assessed). This is particularly true of someone versed in the principles of what is sometimes called 'new pay', a set of theories and practices that highlights pay's role as a management tool and emphasises the importance of aligning employee behaviours with business strategy. Figure 6.1 compares 'new pay' with more traditional pay systems.

Traditional pay systems focus on measuring job inputs, specifically time and ability. They work well in combination with job evaluation, described in a well-known handbook of human resource management practice as 'a systematic process for defining the relative worth or size of jobs within an organisation in order to establish internal relativities and provide the basis for designing an equitable grade and pay structure, grading jobs in the structure and managing relativities'.[77] Remuneration is predominantly in the form of fixed pay (wages and salaries), along with pensions and benefits, sometimes accompanied by

Figure 6.1: Traditional pay versus new pay

	Traditional pay	New pay
Basis	Input-focused – based on job description time inputs	Output-focused – based on person and performance
Composition	Predominantly fixed pay, possibly with small variable – pay add-ons	Fixed pay, bonuses and long-term incentives
Market position	Based on internal labour markets; external fit not emphasised	Based on external labour markets; less emphasis on internal fit
Benchmark/ equity focus	Internal market, external market only at main ports of entry	External market
Hierarchy/ grade structure	Significant hierarchy required – suits traditional organisation structures	Minimal hierarchy required – suits flat organisation structures
Psychological contract	Loyalty and entitlement	Employability and performance

bonuses, which would in turn be typically small relative to fixed pay. New pay (which is, incidentally, now quite an old concept, as it dates back to the early 1990s[78]) focuses on outputs and involves a much greater proportion of variable pay linked to performance. New pay is now quite widely supported and appears to be deeply intuitive – people generally have a sense that desert is a form of 'natural justice'. To a philosopher, however, the idea that distributive justice is connected with merit or desert is far from clear. In the way that philosophers do, they would pose a number of difficult questions. What constitutes 'desert'? Is the intention to reward effort, ability, performance or what? Should a distinction be made between innate ability, or capabilities that a person has worked hard to acquire? How can some people deserve more than others when their contribution depends upon a greater natural talent? As Ronald Dworkin has pointed out, 'no one has control over their natural endowments, although they can, of course, choose which of these endowments to develop and exercise'.[79] If some people deserve rewards, it is surely only on the basis of characteristics for which they can be held responsible, namely their efforts and choices. Is the intention to reward only virtuous abilities like honesty and reliability, or also to reward vice-like abilities like ruthlessness (which is sometimes seen as a positive quality in a management context) or greed? Consider the case of two postgraduates, let's call them Janet and John, with PhDs in physics. John joins an investment bank as a quant trader and makes huge sums of money for his bank and for himself. Janet becomes a research scientist and earns a modest salary. Can John really be said to be more deserving than Janet, especially if he is motivated primarily by greed?

Another question: is the objective to reward past performance or to incentivise future performance? A manager who awards a bonus to an employee in recognition for meeting a high sales target might be trying to encourage other employees to strive to meet equivalent sales targets in the future, which strictly speaking has got nothing to do with desert.

Focusing on performance raises another set of questions. Does it matter if performance is by accident? For example, at time T_1 person X might mean to do A but accidentally does B. At time T_2 it turns out that B is a better outcome than A. Does X deserve to be rewarded? Similarly, what if performance is a matter of luck? A true story – I have very poor eyesight, and once, in a competition with my then-teenaged sons, hit the bullseye on a shooting range even though I was aiming at the wrong target. I claimed credit, of course, but this (as the boys pointed out to me) was hardly justified.

Last but not least, how is desert to be measured? In some circumstances this is easier than others (for example, hitting a financial target, or not, when the focus is on operational performance). But in an organisational context are financial targets necessarily the best measures? And is it absolute or relative performance, for example in comparison with past performance or comparable businesses, that really matters?

We will return to the measurement problem in due course, but first a brief history of philosophical thinking about desert.

A brief history of desert

The idea that distributive justice should be based on merit has a long history. Greek society associated virtue with both status and success. Homeric heroes were virtuous because of their high standing in society and because they were successful. It was a form of strict meritocracy – what mattered was winning and continuing to win. However, there was an asymmetry between distributive and retributive justice, between reward for success and punishment for failure. The Athenians were haunted by the idea of strict liability. Oedipus was punished for committing patricide, albeit that he did so unknowingly and in self-defence, and for then marrying his father's widow, Jocasta, who turned out to be his birth mother. Fate intervenes and trumps any mitigating factors.

Intention was, at least for the Greeks, at best of secondary importance. It is only later, perhaps in the 17th and 18th centuries, that success and failure, so acclaimed in a strict meritocracy, were qualified by good and bad intentions, a more desert-based scheme. By the 19th and 20th centuries, liberal values, influenced perhaps by developments in the social sciences that drew attention to the importance of heredity and environment – genes and memes, if you like – the notion that desert is the primary basis for determining what constitutes distributive justice had become heavily qualified, certainly among moral philosophers.[80]

We can see in this brief and admittedly somewhat Western-biased history some of the main features of, and questions raised by, the idea of desert as a distributive scheme. Are we to reward success only (a strict meritocracy) or right intentions (a more qualified desert-based system)? To what extent are distributive justice (is reward deserved?) and retributive justice (is punishment warranted?) symmetrical or asymmetrical systems? Is rewarding desert simply a matter of natural justice, or is it also in some way instrumental – does hard work deserve to be rewarded because it will encourage others to work hard? Is desert individualistic (focused only on certain people or events) or patterned, a distributive scheme applicable to a group, company, or society as a whole? Do relativities matter, and how do we assess comparability? It is also important to distinguish between desert or merit-based schemes, and rights – if Joe is a Band 10, and Band 10s are paid between £60,000 and £75,000, then Joe may have a right to receive between £60,000 and £75,000, but that does not necessarily mean that he deserves it.

Desert-based schemes retain an intuitive appeal. The Scottish philosopher W.D. Ross puts it like this:

> If we compare two imaginary states of the universe, alike in the total amounts of vice and virtue and of pleasure and pain present in the two, but in one of which the virtuous were all happy and the vicious miserable,

> while in the other the virtuous were miserable and the
> vicious happy, very few people would hesitate to say that
> the first was a much better state of the universe than the
> second.[81]

This concept of individual desert plays an important role in our practice of linking merit with responsibility and respect, so that moral philosophers who entirely discount desert are sometimes viewed as being intolerably unrealistic by the public. Nevertheless, the idea of justice as desert, a thesis held for centuries as a component of sound moral and political theory, has been rejected by many modern moral and political philosophers.

A notable exception is the Oxford political philosopher David Miller, who we met briefly in Chapter 1. Miller advances a relatively sophisticated, pluralistic theory of distributive justice. He divides human action into three spheres of activity. The first involves relationships in community, when people 'share a common identity as members of a relatively stable group with a common ethos'. Miller describes the second sphere as 'instrumental association'. Here:

> people relate to one another in a utilitarian manner –
> each has aims and purposes that can best be realised by
> collaboration with others. Economic relations are the
> paradigm case of this mode.

The third sphere is based on citizenship. Miller argues that in modern liberal democracies people are related to each other not just through local communities and in their instrumental economic relationships but also as fellow citizens with equal rights and equal votes. Anyone who is a full member of the polity is the bearer of a set of rights and obligations that together define their status as citizens.

Miller argues that the ethical distributive systems in each sphere of human activity are different. Within communities the substantive principle of justice is need. Any member of a community who finds themselves in need, whether as a result of bad luck or bad choices, has a reasonable expectation that the community will help out – I will support my neighbour in their time of need, not least because I recognise that I may need my neighbour's help at some time in the future. In the economic sphere the relevant principle of justice is distribution according to desert. The economy will thrive if economic units perform well. Organisational performance is optimised when human resources are appropriately incentivised and rewarded. The output of most enterprises can be measured in monetary terms and participants should receive by way of fixed or variable pay a share of the total economic output for which they can be held to be responsible. Within society the primary distributive principle of citizenship association is equality. Citizens who lack the resources necessary to play their part as full members of society have a just claim to have those resources provided. These three spheres of human action and primary modes of distributive justice are illustrated in Figure 6.2.

If we focus now specifically on the economic sphere, Miller is realistic about some of the difficulties posed by a distribution system based upon desert. What is just is substantially, he believes, culturally defined. It is not possible to arrive at a single system of distributive justice by pure reason. Nor are ethical facts intuitive. Principles of justice are therefore neither universal nor natural. Instead they are defined by the local institutions in which we operate – 'institutions' here meaning the regular patterns of human action in which people are assigned rights and obligations, encouraged to behave in one way or another, expected to perform certain tasks, and have reasonable expectations of particular

Figure 6.2: David Miller's pluralistic view of distributive justice

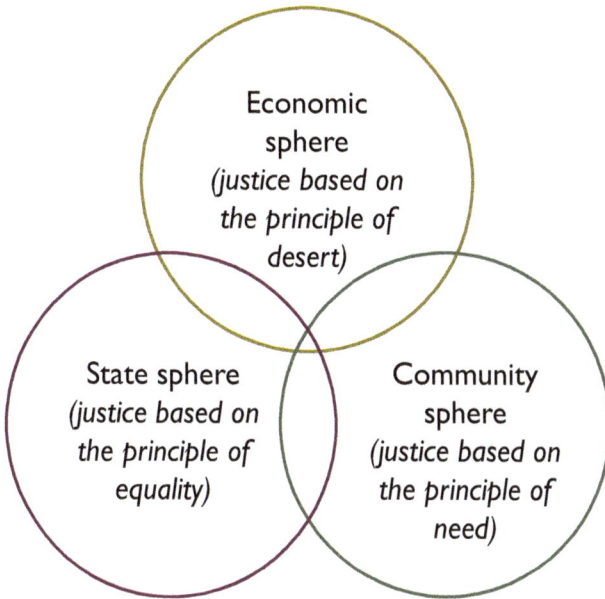

Economic sphere
(justice based on the principle of desert)

State sphere
(justice based on the principle of equality)

Community sphere
(justice based on the principle of need)

kinds of reward as a result. The economic historian Douglas North describes institutions as 'the humanly devised constraints that structure political, economic and social interaction', which 'consist of both informal constraints (sanctions, taboos, customs, traditions, and codes of conduct) and formal rules (constitutions, laws, property rights)'. He continues: 'throughout history, institutions have been devised by human beings to create order and reduce uncertainty in exchange'. 'They are,' he says, with a glancing reference to economic game theory, 'the rules of the game.'[82]

Miller therefore argues that, in the context of the institutions that form the bedrock of Western liberal democracy, pay scales in industry are a compromise between what may generally be regarded as fair reward differentials between workers with different skills and responsibilities and the bargaining power wielded by different sections of the workforce. Wages are compensation for carrying out demanding jobs. Alternatively, but not inconsistently, they are incentives that encourage workers to take on difficult jobs, thus enabling the economy to operate efficiently, which otherwise, absent forced labour or some other type of coercion, it would not.

This approach is entirely consistent with Miller's comment, which I quoted in Chapter 1, that:

> empirical evidence should play a significant role in justifying a normative theory of justice, or to put it another way, that such a theory is to be tested, in part, by its correspondence with our evidence concerning everyday beliefs about justice.[83]

However, there remains one significant issue for the meritocrats who seek to justify high executive pay by reference to desert.

The measurement problem

Desert theories assume, one way or another, that a person's reward should depend on the value that that person contributes through their work activity. 'Value' might in theory be measured in a number of different ways, but, given the context, the most prominent theory of desert identifies the value of a worker's contribution with its 'market value'. According to general equilibrium theory, in an efficient market economy product prices and wages are connected. Demand and supply determine product prices and the quantity of goods sold. This helps to determine the demand for the labour required to make the relevant product, which in turn, in conjunction with the supply of labour (the amount of appropriately skilled labour that is available), determines the price of labour, that is, the market clearing wage. The political philosopher Michael Walzer sums it up like this.

> The market, if it is free, gives each person exactly what he deserves. ... The goods and services we provide are valued by potential customers in such-and-such a way, and these values are aggregated by the market, which determines what price we receive. And that price is our desert, for it expresses the only worth our goods and services can have, the worth they actually have for other people.[84]

Executive remuneration is inextricably bound up with market value in another way. Senior executives employed by quoted companies typically receive a significant part of their total rewards in a way that is directly or indirectly related to the market value of the shares of their employing companies. They may be paid partly in shares or share options. Their bonuses may be related to share price performance.

One way or another, 'desert' and 'market value' appear to be closely connected. However, not all philosophers accept that market values and ethics are interrelated. The neoliberal economist F.A. Hayek argues that, as prices determined in product markets are neither 'just' nor 'unjust', so distributive justice is not a feature of wages determined by demand and supply in labour markets. Hayek quotes with approval the philosopher R.G. Collingwood, who said:

> It is impossible for prices to be fixed by any reference to the idea of justice or any other moral conception. A just price, a just wage ... is a contradiction in terms. The question of what a person ought to get in return for his goods and labour is a question absolutely devoid of meaning. The only questions are what he can get in

> return for his goods or labour, and whether he ought to
> sell them at all.[85]

Nor, presumably, according to the same logic, can share prices
determined in capital markets be said to be 'just' or 'unjust'. 'Value'
in an economic sense has nothing to do with value in an ethical
sense. Prices, according to Hayek, are the result of the 'spontane-
ous order' that emerges in free market economies. Markets are
part of an economic game in which only the conduct of the players, and not the result, can be said to be just or unjust. Hayek,
incidentally, had no particular problem with this – the absence
of distributive justice in labour markets is, as far as he was concerned, much less important than the loss of liberty that would
result if governments intervened in any substantive way.[86]

In defence of the market value theory of desert, we might argue
that wages do not just 'spontaneously emerge' in labour markets,
as Hayek is perhaps suggesting. Employee rewards in modern
market economies are determined through complex systems of
comparison that take place both within and between organisations. Within organisations, HR departments spend a great deal
of time evaluating performance – rating and ranking employees and establishing appropriate differentials between different
grades. They also benchmark their wage levels against rewards
offered by competitors in the labour market, especially for occupations and job grades that are subject to high turnover. Trade
unions also gather data and negotiate with employers on behalf
of their members. Labour markets are, in the words of the Nobel
Prize-winning economist Robert Solow, 'social institutions' as
well as components of the economic system. According to David
Miller, market-based criteria that determine wage levels in efficient labour markets will generally be accepted as a non-arbitrary

public standard, and therefore as a legitimate part of society's institutional framework.

In summary, as the philosopher Robert Young says in the journal *Ethics*, 'private enterprise under perfectly competitive economic conditions would produce deserved outcomes'.[87] Neo-classical economic theory is committed to the idea that in a free market economy everyone gets his or her deserts. Notwithstanding this, as Young goes on to say,

> to the very great extent that perfect competition does not hold sway there can be very little comfort for supporters of desert-based distributions that in the theoretical model it does [produce deserved outcomes].

I have already made the case in Chapter 1 that executive labour markets are not efficient. Indeed, there are good reasons to believe that high executive pay is an example of market failure, a topic to which I will turn again in the next chapter.

To sum up

Meritocrats believe in the importance of equal opportunities regardless, for example, of differences in gender or race. They would want there to be a safety net to protect the least well paid members of society, to ensure that they are able to live a dignified life. However, the most important criteria for determining differences in pay are performance and ability. Mechanisms that assess performance and determine what is paid on the basis of merit are most likely to produce efficient outcomes, which will in turn be in the best interests of individuals and communities.

CHAPTER 7

Free marketeers

Free marketeers believe that economic efficiency is the main criterion for determining how income should be allocated. They endorse the claim that talented people deserve to receive economic advantages and that everyone should have the opportunity to demonstrate their ability, although their focus is on well-functioning markets and the efficient allocation of scarce resources. In their responses to the survey these executives said things like:

- 'Without the rich, there is no wealth creation.'
- 'I don't think that income should be redistributed automatically if the recipients of the redistributed income are not willing to contribute to society.'
- 'People will take advantage of redistribution if standards are not set.'

How to cite this book chapter:
Pepper, A. 2022. *If You're So Ethical, Why Are You So Highly Paid?: Ethics, Inequality and Executive Pay.* London: LSE Press. Pp. 81–90.
DOI: https://doi.org/10.31389/lsepress/eth License: CC BY-NC

- 'I strongly believe members of society should be motivated to work and that income redistribution removes this motivation.'
- 'Let free markets reign! I want a society where people are free to win according to their skills, abilities, efforts and contributions – I accept that in such a society, there will be some losers.'

Robert Nozick and entitlement theory

As G.A. Cohen and Ronald Dworkin were near contemporaries at Oxford, so John Rawls and Robert Nozick were colleagues at Harvard, yet two scholars with more different political philosophies are hard to imagine. While Rawls was a rather unflashy liberal, Nozick was a somewhat flamboyant libertarian. He issued a fundamental challenge to Rawls's principle that social and economic inequalities should be arranged so that they are of the greatest benefit to the least-advantaged members of society. Nozick's work traces its heritage back to John Locke's *Second Treatise on Government* (1689), especially the ideas of 'self-ownership' and the protection of property. Nozick draws upon the Kantian principle that people should be treated as an end in themselves, not merely as a means to an end, an idea that he calls 'the separateness of persons'. In order to be different 'ends in themselves', Kant observed that people must be separate beings whose integrity (in the sense of their 'wholeness' or 'unity') must be respected. Benefits to some larger entity, such as 'the common good' or society as a whole, cannot be used as a justification for violating the rights of individual persons.

In *Anarchy, State, and Utopia*, which was published in 1974, Nozick contests the main argument in Rawls's *A Theory of Justice* by advancing an alternative 'entitlement theory'. Stated briefly, his argument proceeds by advancing three propositions. The first proposition is that a person, X, whose holding of social and economic goods has been acquired justly (that is, from a demonstrably just starting point) is entitled to that holding. The second proposition is that a person, Y, who acquires a holding of social and economic goods by a just transfer from person X, is entitled to that holding. The third proposition is that no one is entitled to a holding except by repeated applications of propositions one and two.

Nozick continues: 'the complete principle of distributive justice would say simply that a distribution is just if everyone is entitled to their holdings under the distribution'. Nozick expands on this argument in a number of ways. Imagine a distribution of goods D_1 that is demonstrably just; for example, under D_1 all persons $P_1...P_n$ might have equal holdings that had been freely provided without any hint of coercion. This distribution can be thought of as broadly equivalent to the 'original position' in Rawls. Imagine then that persons $P_2...P_n$ decide to transfer economic goods representing part of their original holdings to P_1 under transfers which are freely and voluntarily made. Therefore it must be the case, says Nozick, that the resulting distribution of goods D_2 is just, even if P_1's holding is materially greater than the holdings of $P_2...P_n$. He illustrates this argument with the story of Wilt Chamberlain, a famous American basketball player of the 1960s–1970s.

> Suppose that Wilt Chamberlain is greatly in demand by basketball teams, being a great gate attraction. ... He signs the following sort of contract with a team. In each home game, twenty five cents from the price of each ticket of admission goes to him. ... The season starts, and people cheerfully attend his team's games;

they buy their tickets, each time dropping a separate twenty five cents of their admission price into a special box with Chamberlain's name on it. They are excited about seeing him play; it is worth the total admission price to them. Let us suppose that in one season one million persons attend his home games, and Wilt Chamberlain winds up with $250,000, a much larger sum than the average income and larger even than anyone else has. Is he entitled to this income? Is this new distribution D_2 unjust? If so, why?[88]

Nozick's contention is that the distribution of income that leaves Wilt Chamberlain in receipt of $250,000 is just, regardless of the fact that his income is higher than that of his peers and (presumably) much higher than that of many of his supporters. Nor is there any evidence, as Rawls would have it, that 'the difference in expectation is to the advantage of the representative man who is worse off'. The distribution is just simply because Wilt Chamberlain is *entitled* to his share of income and wealth. Nozick's argument is essentially the same as the one the Edwardian novelist E.M. Forster puts into the mouth of one of his upper-middle-class characters in *Howards End*, published in 1910:

You do admit that, if wealth was divided up equally, in a few years' time there would be rich and poor again just the same. The hard-working man would come to the top, the wastrel sink to the bottom.[89]

It is important to recognise at this point that none of the four clusters is fully aligned with entitlement theory, and I include a reference to Nozick here solely because of his importance in the general scheme of distributive justice, and also because, perhaps, free marketeers come closest to the libertarian thinking of Nozick. It is an important argument, and one that underpins much contemporary business thinking about the importance of 'talent'. Some people possess enormous talent, so the argument goes, and have the ability to generate superior value, and there is nothing unjust about others choosing to pay for this talent if they agree that it creates superior value.

However, entitlement theory is susceptible to an important counter-argument. In part this is associated with Ronald Dworkin's distinction between option luck and brute luck. Wilt Chamberlain's ability to command a much larger than average income was primarily the result of his superior innate ability and because the institutional environment allowed him to cash in on his talent. He had the good fortune to be endowed with a set of physical characteristics – speed, strength and height (he was 7ft 1in tall) – that helped to make him a great basketball player. To reward him for this is to reward his good fortune or, as Dworkin would have it, 'brute luck'. Of course, some part of Chamberlain's superior performance is due to effort in the way he used his natural endowments: no doubt his employers would want to reward him for this, and effort is a positive moral application; however the 'star' quality is something he was born with and arguably, according to Dworkin's theory of distributive justice, should be of no moral consequence. But to Nozick a person's right to make free transfers trumps all other considerations.

The Canadian philosopher David Gauthier makes much the same point in a slightly different way, using the star ice hockey player Wayne Gretzky in his thought experiment – as Gauthier says, while Americans revere basketball stars, Canadians hero-worship ice hockey players.

> There is an additional demand for the unique hockey skills of Wayne Gretzky, expressed by the fact that

> half-empty arenas fill up when Gretzky and the Edmonton Oilers come to town. There is no substitute available to meet this demand. Gretzky is therefore in a position to extract payment for his services over and above the cost to him, including the opportunity cost, of supplying those services; he is in a position to extract factor rent. Gretzky would, quite likely, be willing to play hockey for a lower salary than he receives; the difference between the least amount that would induce him to play as well as he does and his actual remuneration is then his rent.[90]

Gauthier's argument is that there is nothing in the principles of self-ownership and the protection of property, upon which entitlement theory is based, which provide moral justification for economic rents. Gretzky is free to play hockey and can rightly expect to cover all his costs in so doing, including the opportunity cost of alternative employment. But this does not justify price gouging. It is only right, says Gauthier, that the additional surplus that arises only because of Gretzky's interaction with other people should be shared in some way among the people who generate the surplus.

This last point is explained even more clearly by Joseph Heath, another Canadian philosopher, who we met briefly in Chapter 2. To understand Heath's argument, we need to know something about the 'market failures approach' to business ethics that he pioneered.

The market failures approach

The last of the six perspectives on distributive justice that provide the foundations for the research addressed in this book is the market failures approach to business ethics.[91] Its main proponent, Joseph Heath, argues as follows. The principal ethical objective of a free market capitalist economy is Pareto optimal efficiency, because, if this objective is achieved, then societal wealth is maximised, and provided there is an appropriate mechanism for allocating wealth (admittedly a big proviso), then societal welfare will also be maximised. Market failures (when the market does not operate effectively, for example, where there is inequality of bargaining power, resulting in imperfect competition) undermine Pareto optimal efficiency. Deliberately exploiting market failures, as occurs, for example, in monopolies or oligopolies, goes against the efficiency principle and is therefore unethical. Therefore, business ethics should focus attention on instances when markets do not operate efficiently, for example when there are market failures, monopolies, price gouging, economic rents and negative externalities. Thus, Heath contends that economic rents arising in circumstances like the Wilt Chamberlain and Wayne Gretzky cases are not morally justified.

Underpinning the market failures approach is a fundamental belief in the efficacy of market economies, the economic system in which decisions regarding investment, production and distribution are determined by the laws of supply and demand, guided by the price mechanism. Market economies range from minimally regulated laissez faire systems to more interventionist forms where governments play an active role in regulating markets, correcting market failures, and promoting general welfare. I say this is an axiomatic belief only because the philosophers who advocate the market failures approach to business ethics take the efficacy of market economies as read, but it is a belief that is supported by an enormous amount of empirical evidence. One need only consider the vast increase in GDP per capita that has been seen in market economies since the change from feudalism to capitalism, which can be located somewhere in the 18th century.

Figure 7.1: GDP per capita in the US and UK, 1700–2000

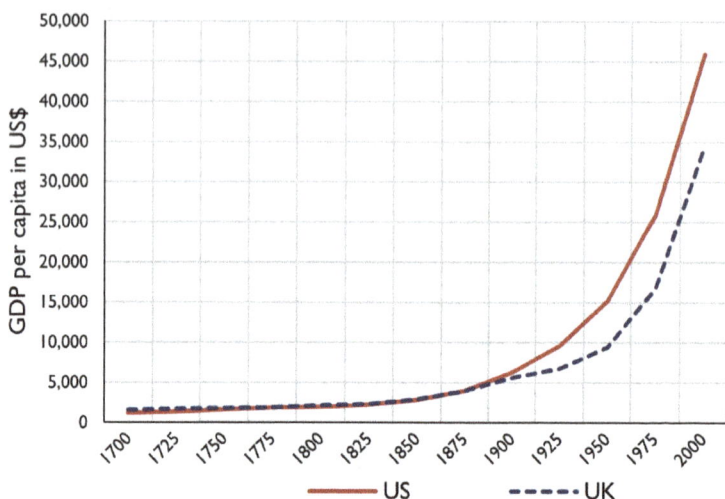

Figure 7.1 shows how GDP per capita has grown exponentially in the US and the UK since that time.

In 1700, GDP per capita in US dollars at early 21st-century exchange rates and purchasing power parity amounted to around $1,200 in the US and $1,600 in the UK. By 1900 this had risen to around $6,000 in both countries. In 2000, GDP per capita was nearly $46,000 in the and $35,000 in the UK. These are staggering changes, if you think about it, and do appear to justify faith in the economic effectiveness of market economies.

However, the market failures approach is not a comprehensive theory of justice, nor does it aspire to be. It does not deal with ethical issues that have no connections with markets: is there such a thing as a just war in which the good to be achieved outweighs the evils involved? Do human embryos have a right to life? Do I have a right to protest that trumps legal restrictions placed on gathering in large crowds during a public health emergency? Nor is an efficient market necessarily in all circumstances an ethical one –

one could imagine, for example, an efficient market for trading in human organs, which we would judge to be unethical for all sorts of reasons. The Cambridge economist Joan Robinson – no fan, it has to be said, of free market economics – once put it rather forcefully like this:

> The doctrines of laissez faire are very attractive, not only to those who gained most directly from the market system. If the economy is a self-regulating mechanism and economics a system of scientific laws, moral and political problems are excluded from it. Questions of social justice do not arise, all the operations of public administration are to be strictly neutral between interested parties. Ethics can be discussed on Sunday. It is considered unsound, soft-headed and unpatriotic to bring it in to week-day business. As soon as we recognise that the market, by its very nature, is necessarily a scene of conflicting interests, every element in it becomes a moral and political problem.[92]

Nevertheless, the market failures approach is extraordinarily helpful because of the way that it focuses the attention of business ethicists on specific market situations. It is particularly relevant in the present context because, as I have previously argued, very high executive compensation has many of the hallmarks of a market failure. It is an important counter to Nozick's 'Wilt Chamberlain' argument, which, as Joseph Heath and David Gauthier have pointed out, is about economic rents, and is therefore susceptible to the market failures approach critique.

Thus, for present purposes, when it comes to executive pay, the market failures principle of distributive justice can be set out in the following terms. The right distribution of income is that which leads to an efficient allocation of labour. Income is the price paid for labour. Under ideal conditions, market prices carry information about the relative scarcity of resources, thereby allowing us to allocate resources to where they can be put to their most valuable use. We should try to see to it that wages are free from distortions, so that they carry information about relative scarcity, and labour markets can operate efficiently. However, labour markets are often far from perfect, especially where small number conditions apply. In such circumstances it is not right to appeal to 'market forces' when markets fail and individuals are able to extract rents. We must look to other ways of determining what is and is not fair in such cases.

It will probably be apparent that there is a close relationship between the market failures approach to business ethics and what I described in Chapter 2 as the market failure hypothesis when it comes to executive pay. If we cannot appeal to market efficiency when it comes to high pay, that is to say, if labour markets for top executives are not efficient, then we may need to look for some kind of ethical intervention.

To sum up

Free marketeers are the ultimate believers in the efficiency of markets, including labour markets. People should be paid for their ability and achievements. It is right to reward differential performance. Free marketeers believe in equal opportunities for all, regardless of gender or race, but it is perfectly acceptable to differentiate on the basis of capabilities and contribution. However, there are limits – the accumulation of extraordinary wealth as a consequence of market imperfections would not be condoned by the free marketeer's code of ethics. They would not say that 'anything goes'. Markets should be made to work efficiently, and people should behave in such a way that they do.

CHAPTER 8

If executives are so ethical, why are they so highly paid?

Less arresting is the opposite case, in which people strive to govern their behaviour by (what are in fact) just principles, but ignorance, or the obduracy of wholly external circumstances, or collective action problems, or self-defeatingness of the kinds studied by Derek Parfit, or something else which I have not thought of, frustrates their intention, so that the distribution remains unjust.

G.A. Cohen (2000)[93]

In the previous four chapters I have described the ethical beliefs of a representative sample of business executives from across the world by clustering the data into four sets or types: welfare liberals, relational egalitarians, meritocrats and free marketeers. Alongside these four types I have explained the normative theories of six philosophers whose ideas underpin the executives' beliefs about

How to cite this book chapter:
Pepper, A. 2022. *If You're So Ethical, Why Are You So Highly Paid?: Ethics, Inequality and Executive Pay.* London: LSE Press. Pp. 91–110.
    DOI: https://doi.org/10.31389/lsepress/eth License: CC BY-NC

distributive justice: the big four – Rawls (maximin, or 'the difference principle'), Cohen (egalitarianism), Dworkin (luck egalitarianism) and Nozick (entitlement) – along with Frankfurt (sufficiency) and Heath (efficiency, or the 'market failures approach').

If the data from our survey are to be believed, and I believe that they should be, then senior executives are not in the main the greedy ethical egoists of popular culture. Certainly it is true that many of them, especially the free marketeers, believe that it is perfectly ethical to allow markets to determine economically efficient outcomes. Furthermore, most, especially the merito-crats, believe that it is quite proper to reward people differentially, having regard to their effort, ability and the demands of the job. Nevertheless, many, including relational egalitarians and welfare liberals, believe in the principle of sufficiency, that in a civilised society everyone has the right to an income that is sufficient for a dignified life, and that companies, not just governments, have responsibilities in this respect. Some, notably the welfare liber-als, subscribe to the Rawlsian difference principle (maximin) that differential incomes can only be justified to the extent that this is necessary to maximise the welfare of the worst-off members of society. Relatively few subscribe to Robert Nozick's entitlement theory, which justifies extraordinary differences in income and wealth on the basis of self-ownership and property rights.

The four clusters encapsulate the everyday beliefs of business executives in our sample. While they constitute a range of differ-ent ethical positions within the field of possibilities, they are all coherent and internally consistent. The executives commented in the narrative part of the survey that they believe companies have a direct role to play in bringing about distributive justice through their policies and procedures. They do not think that matters of distributive justice should simply be left for governments to deal with, for example through the tax system, although they do accept that governments have an important role to play in ensuring that we do live in a just society. They also believe that there is currently a significant justice deficit at both society and company levels.

In a characteristically provocative book title, G.A. Cohen posed the question 'if you're an egalitarian, why are you so rich?' He might, with some justification, pose a similar question here: 'if executives are so ethical, why are they so highly paid?' Hence the variations on the title of Cohen's book in the chapter heading and the book title. To put this question in another way, why has the business community allowed inflation in executive pay, increasing differentials, and the consequential rise in inequality to occur?

The answer, I believe, lies in the social and institutional systems, involving company executives, shareholders and boards of directors, which have evolved over the last 35 to 40 years – specifically in a misplaced confidence in the efficiency of labour markets, in the dangers of a persuasive but ultimately flawed academic idea combined with a poor choice of mechanism design, in a sociological concept called 'isomorphism', and in the way politicians have responded to the problems associated with high executive pay.

In *The Fifth Discipline*, a remarkable book published in 1990, Peter Senge, who was at the time director of the Systems Thinking and Organizational Learning Program at the Sloan School of Management, Massachusetts Institute of Technology, describes how organisations can be analysed as systems using a set of principles developed over the course of the 20th century from disciplines as diverse as engineering, management and both the natural and social sciences. Systems thinking makes particular use of ideas about feedback loops from cybernetic theory and servomechanisms (automatic devices used to correct performance by means of error-correction signals) from control engineering.

Feedback comes in two forms. Positive, reinforcing or amplifying feedback (choose your terminology) causes systems to run faster and faster and is an engine of growth. Negative, balancing or stabilising feedback slows things down, corrects errors and makes sure that systems remain in a state of equilibrium.[94] Senge also talks about dynamic complexity, situations in which relationships between cause and effect are uncertain and time effects are unclear, as well as circles of causality, where effects become causes in repeating cycles of action.

One of Peter Senge's most important insights is that systems that are rich in amplifying feedback are inherently unstable. In the absence of control mechanisms and negative feedback, such systems run faster and faster and eventually lurch out of control. Senge cites the US–USSR arms race that took place between 1950 and 1990 as an example of such a system – one side increased its stock of nuclear weapons; the other side perceived an enhanced threat; this caused it to increase its supply of nuclear weapons; the first side perceived an enhanced threat, causing it to further increase its stock of nuclear weapons; so the cycle continued.

It is my contention that executive compensation systems in the US and UK have for some time been unstable – remuneration programmes characterised by amplifying feedback mechanisms, such as the remuneration committee's dilemma, without adequate control mechanisms to dampen down pay inflation. The result has been systematic market failure and payment of economic rents.

The causes of market failure

'My remuneration,' said the CEO of a large UK-quoted company in response to a question at his company's annual general meeting, 'is determined by market forces. There really is nothing more to say on the matter.'[95] I explained in Chapter 2 what is wrong with this argument. While the medieval schoolmen might have believed that the laws of supply and demand can determine what is and is not a just wage, labour markets are not like other commodity markets and often behave in idiosyncratic ways. 'Labour is not a commodity like fish', as Nobel Prize-winning economist Robert Solow once said.[96] This is particularly true of specialist roles where labour is not homogenous, when there are a limited number of suitable candidates, and where information is incomplete. The concept of 'talent markets', as these fields are sometimes known, is something of a myth. When it comes to CEOs, footballers, basketball players and ice hockey stars, labour markets are just not very efficient.

A flawed idea

The flawed idea is agency theory. I explained in Chapter 2 that empirical evidence gathered over the past 35 years has failed to establish a strong statistical link between executive pay and a firm's financial performance, as predicted by agency theory. Most economists now appear to accept that the strongest empirical correlation is between executive pay and firm size. Some economists argue that this is not necessarily inefficient. Big companies are presumably more complex and difficult to run than smaller companies. Big companies must therefore attract the best management talent in order to run efficiently. They should therefore provide the largest pay packets. But there is something unsatisfactory about this argument. To accept ex post that a correlation between CEO pay and company size is an acceptable outcome, when aiming ex ante for a causal connection between CEO pay and firm performance, is a rather weak argument.

An analogy: an absent-minded academic sets off to drive to Edinburgh, where he is speaking at a conference. On the way he takes a wrong turning and ends up in Glasgow instead. On the telephone to the chair of the conference to explain his error, he argues that this is nevertheless an acceptable outcome, as he has still arrived in Scotland. Really? To theorise that a specific set of factors and circumstances will lead to a particular outcome, then to argue after the event that a different outcome is still valid is to my mind self-evidently flawed logic.

The poor choice of mechanism design is the one promoted on the back of agency theory, that senior executives should receive a substantial part of their remuneration in the form of share-based performance-related long-term incentives, or LTIPs for short. Joseph Heath points out, in an essay entitled 'The Uses and Abuses of Agency Theory', that many long-term highly leveraged performance-linked incentive plans are of 'baroque complexity'. Executives attach high psychological discounts for such complexity, as well as for time, risk and uncertainly. It means that, quite reasonably, they attach less value to their LTIP awards than the LTIP's apparent face value and economic cost, creating a psychological value gap, illustrated in Figure 8.1.

One of the consequences of the value gap is that remuneration committees increase the size of LTIP awards in order to compensate executives for the perceived loss of value. This increases the economic cost to the company and the size of the eventual payouts under the LTIP arrangement, fuelling inflation in executive pay, an unsatisfactory and expensive consequence of a flawed mechanism design.

Figure 8.1: The LTIP (long-term incentive plan) value gap

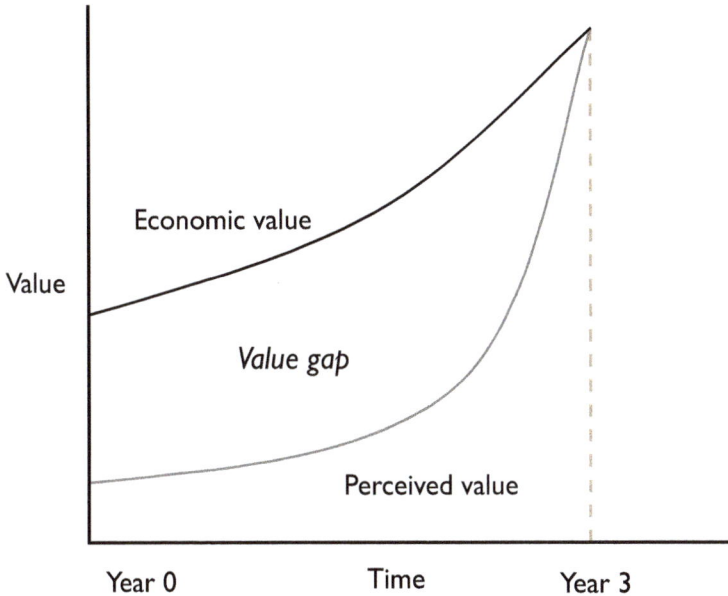

Isomorphism

In sociology, 'isomorphism' describes a process whereby social practices or entities come to develop similar structures or forms. In a classic paper, 'The Iron Cage Revisited: Institutional Isomorphism and Collective Rationality in Organizational Fields', published in 1983, American sociologists Paul J. DiMaggio and Walter W. Powell explain how organisations and work processes become similar over time as a result of a process that they call 'isomorphism' but which might equally well, in plain English, be described simply as 'copying'. DiMaggio and Powell identify three different types of isomorphism: *mimetic* isomorphism (think 'imitation'), which they say is a standard response to uncertainty; *coercive* isomorphism, which is the result of political pressure and the search for legitimacy; and *normative* isomorphism, which is associated with professional standards and the search for 'best practice'. All three are rooted in bounded rationality.

The first public company in the UK to establish an LTIP was Prudential in the early 1990s, followed soon after by Reuters and British Telecom. In 1995 the Greenbury Report, which had been commissioned in response to public and shareholder concerns about directors' remuneration, in effect mandated the use of LTIPs when it recommended that 'the performance-related elements of remuneration should be designed to align the interests of directors and shareholders and to give directors keen incentives to perform at the highest levels'. The Greenbury Report went on: 'remuneration committees should consider whether their directors should be eligible for benefits under long-term incentive schemes' and recommended, rather cryptically, that 'traditional share option schemes should be weighed against other kinds of long-term incentive scheme'. The Association of British Insurers and National Association of Pension Funds, two trade associations whose members at the time together held a substantial proportion of shares listed on the London Stock Exchange, went further, issuing guidelines that prescribed the terms on which LTIPs should be issued, encouraging phased grants, vesting periods of a minimum of three years, and the application of rigorous financial performance targets. During the same period there was marked growth in the use of pay consultants, such as New Bridge Street Consultants and Towers Perrin, which advised companies on 'best practice' when it came to the design of executive reward strategies, further encouraging the use of LTIPs to align the interests of shareholders and executives.[97]

All three types of isomorphism have been exhibited in the adoption of LTIPs as a standard component of executive packages by UK listed companies – plans for performance-related long-term incentives were copied by one company after another, as they tried to respond to increasing public disquiet about published levels of directors' pay. Companies have been pressurised into conforming with new regulations and codes of practice, and encouraged to follow 'best practice' frameworks recommended by remuneration consultants. As a result, the prevalence of LTIPs in FTSE 100 companies increased rapidly. By 2020 the vast majority of FTSE 100 companies had LTIPs, which represented over 51 per cent of the value of total CEO rewards. And yet all along LTIPs were, for reasons I have already explained, contributing to inflation in executive pay.

Government response to high executive pay

Governments often recognise the need to intervene in cases of market failure. Yet, when it comes to executive pay, direct intervention, for example by taxation or mandatory pay caps, has been relatively unusual.[98] While politicians have sometimes had quite a lot to say about high pay, they have tended to leave it to shareholders to solve the problem. Successive governments in the UK have acknowledged 'a widespread perception that executive pay has become increasingly disconnected from both the pay of ordinary working people and the underlying long-term performance of companies'.[99] However, rather than legislating to restrict executive pay, their approach has been to increase disclosure requirements and to encourage investors to take responsibility for moderating pay practices.

The UK was the first country to introduce 'say-on-pay' provisions in 2002 – at the same time it became mandatory for listed companies to publish a directors' remuneration report along with their annual accounts. A further set of provisions relating to the say-on-pay regime was introduced in 2013 when share-holders were granted a triennial binding vote on remuneration policy alongside the annual advisory vote on the directors' remuneration report. These regulations also require companies to set out in a single figure the total remuneration of each person who served as a director during the year, making the remuneration report much easier to understand. This figure includes all salary, bonuses and any other cash payments, taxable benefits, pension contributions, and the market value of any share awards that have vested during the year.

The next step in the evolution of the pay disclosure regime came into effect at the start of 2020, when it became a statutory requirement for UK listed companies with more than 250 employees to disclose annually the ratio of their CEO's pay to the median, upper-quartile and lower-quartile pay of their UK employees. These ratios provide stakeholders, including investors, employees, trade unions and policymakers, with a way of assessing pay distribution and intra-firm pay inequality.

Some of you will have spotted the difficulty here, which I described in Chapter 2 as 'the investors' collective action problem'. While it is all very well for the government to load responsibility for resolving the executive pay problem onto shareholders, an investor owning a small percentage of total stock has no obvious financial incentive to challenge management on excessive pay as the costs of doing so will likely outweigh the potential financial benefits.

Historically, at least until a few years ago, they have been most reluctant to do so. There are now signs of change. Two watershed events that have occurred in the last few years may signal a significant shift in executive pay practices in the UK.

Two watershed events

The first event occurred in April 2017, when Norges Bank Investment Management, which manages the Norwegian Sovereign Wealth Fund on behalf of the Norwegian government, published a research paper identifying a number of issues with LTIP-dominated CEO remuneration practices.[100] The Norwegian Sovereign Wealth Fund is the largest institutional investor on the London Stock Exchange. The issues that were identified included:

- complexity – the fact that LTIPs rely on a set of metrics, often defined relative to an index or group of peer companies, subject to annual changes in targets and performance conditions, so that at any given time an executive might be exposed to multiple generations of LTIPs;
- a misplaced belief in incentives – designing a robust set of metrics for CEOs is notoriously difficult given a multi-year time horizon; there is also a risk that highly engineered incentives might crowd out intrinsic motivation;
- misaligned interests – empirical research indicates that remuneration is most closely correlated with firm size, geography and corporate governance structures, and only weakly correlated with company performance;
- short-term pressures – measurement periods for LTIPs are generally between one and three years, which is shorter than the investment and business cycles in most industries.

The NBIM paper recommended replacing LTIPs with simpler, more robust remuneration models predicated on pay rewards made predominantly in cash, and requiring CEOs to invest a substantial proportion of annual pay in company shares. It concluded:

> This would shift focus onto the impact that the *holding* of shares has on aligning incentives, rather than the *award* of shares. Remuneration would be less variable on paper, but the exposure to the long-term success of the company in the stock market would be less ambiguous. (Emphasis in original.)

The second watershed event occurred in 2018, when the Weir Group plc, a publicly listed Scottish engineering company, replaced its LTIP with a restricted share plan. The new programme removed the performance conditions that had previously attached to the LTIP. The quid pro quo was a reduction in the size of the award and an extended period over which the restricted shares were to vest. The specific details of the new plan were as follows:

- The face value of the restricted stock award was 50 per cent lower than previous grants made under the LTIP.
- The three-year performance-based formula was replaced with a five-year time-based vesting schedule of 50 per cent after three years, 25 per cent after four years and a further 25 per cent after five years.
- After vesting, the formerly restricted shares must be held for a further two-year period, so that the combined vesting and holding period amounts to five, six or seven years, depending on which tranche is involved.

Vesting of the restricted shares was subject to further downwards adjustment at the discretion of the remuneration committee in the event that this is deemed necessary to 'better reflect the underlying performance of the company'. There were also forfeiture and clawback provisions which may be applied in the event that material errors in the financial statements of the company are found at a later date. Ninety-two per cent of the company's shareholders approved the new programme, the first time a plan based on restricted stock had received such a broad endorsement.

Since the Weir Group introduced its new restricted stock plan, a number of other UK quoted companies have adopted similar plans. These include Kingfisher, BT Group, Burberry and Lloyds Bank. They share similar features. It now seems that new plans will receive shareholder approval provided that:

- any LTIP is eliminated entirely;
- it is replaced by restricted stock;
- the face value of the restricted stock award is 50 per cent or less than the face value of the LTIP;
- the time frame in which the restricted stock vests is at least five years.[101]

The reduction in complexity, risk and uncertainty means that executives value restricted stock more than they value LTIPs. Property rights and a sense of ownership are established at the start, when the restricted stock is awarded, so that the time discount is partially eliminated. The value gap is substantially closed. It is all about perception.

Let's look at an example. The first column in Figure 8.2 is an illustrative CEO compensation package for an average FTSE 100 company, comprising a salary, an annual bonus and an LTIP award – pensions and benefits have been ignored for the purposes of simplicity (although the amounts involved, particularly when it comes to pensions, can be substantial). The second column is the executive's perception of the value of the package, using psychological discount rates of 17 per cent for risk and 33 per cent per annum for time, which empirical research

Figure 8.2: Comparing the performance of long-term incentive plans (LTIPs) versus restricted stock awards (RSAs)

	Compensation package with LTIP (illustrative)		Compensation package with RSA (illustrative)	
	Maximum value	Perceived value	Maximum value	Perceived value[a]
	£'000	£'000	£'000	£'000
Salary	500	500	500	500
Bonus	1,000	555[a]	1,000	555[a]
Bonus % of salary	200%	110%	200%	110%
LTIP	2,000	500[b]	—	—
LTIP % of salary	400%	100%	—	—
RSA	—	—	1,000	625[c]
RSA % of salary	—	—	200%	125%
Total	£3,500	£1,555	£2,500	£1,680

Notes: [a] *Calculation of the perceived value assumes discount rates for risk of 17% and time of 33%.*

[b] *LTIP discounted for risk at 17% p.a. and time of 33% p.a. for three years.*

[c] *RSA discounted for risk at 17% and time at 7% p.a. for an average of four years.*

on executives' preferences has indicated is not untypical.[102] The third column shows a compensation package in which the LTIP has been replaced with a restricted stock award (RSA) with a face value that is 50 per cent less than the face value of the LTIP. The fourth column illustrates the CEO's perceived value of the revised package. Here, as well as discounting for risk at 17 per cent, I have discounted for time at a more normal accounting rate of, say, 7 per cent per annum on the basis that the holder of restricted stock will have a much greater psychological sense of ownership at a much earlier stage than with an LTIP.

You will see that, in my illustrative example, the perceived value of the compensation package that incorporates an award of restricted stock is broadly similar (in fact greater!) than the perceived value of the compensation package based around an LTIP, notwithstanding that the face value has reduced by a third.

Revisiting the investors' collective action problem

We need to take a step back at this point and look again at the relationship between public policy and institutional investors when it comes to executive pay. In his work on the collective action problem, Mancur Olson explains that there are three different types of groups, which he describes as 'privileged', 'intermediate' and 'latent'. In a privileged group the benefits of action are likely to exceed the cost for at least some members of the group so that, other things being equal, collective action is likely to succeed. In a latent group the cost of action is likely to exceed the benefits for all group members so that, other things being equal, the action is likely to fail. Small groups are typically privileged; large groups are typically latent; intermediate groups may behave like privileged or latent groups depending on whether coordination, benefits-sharing and cost-sharing are or are not possible in practice. Olson described large, listed companies as 'quasi-public goods'. Investors with minority holdings are, in effect, participating in, in Olson's typology, latent groups; hence collective action is, on the face of it, unlikely to be successful – so he argued.

So much is clear. However, Olson also recognised that there are circumstances where, notwithstanding the narrow economic equation, collective actions by latent groups are still successful.

Political leadership can sometimes help to overcome collective action problems. 'Political entrepreneurs' seeking to build their own reputations may take responsibility for organising latent groups so that collective action problems are overcome. Governments can use political pressure in order to galvanise latent groups into action. And that indeed is what appears to have happened here. Before 2015, large institutional investors were reluctant to take a position on executive pay. Since then many have actively engaged with companies on the subject. In 2016 Legal & General Investment Management published a position paper called *Mind the Gap*, followed by *Principles of Executive Pay* in 2020.[103] In January 2017 newspapers reported that Blackrock was demanding cuts to executive pay and bonuses in companies in which it was invested. In April 2017 the Norwegian Sovereign Wealth Fund published its thoroughly researched position paper, which urged companies to move towards simpler and more robust remuneration models – one of the two decisive moments identified at the beginning of this chapter. Blackrock issued a further statement in April 2019 on the role of public company shareholders in moderating excess pay.

Some large investors have, in effect, decided to take more responsibility for solving their collective action problem. A focus on stewardship, an inherently ethical concept, has at last come to have at least equal importance alongside financial benefits. Nevertheless, one big problem remains.

Solutions to the remuneration committee's dilemma

This is the remuneration committee's dilemma, the multi-person prisoner's dilemma that I described in Chapter 2, whereby remuneration committees, fearing the risk of paying under the odds and being criticised by shareholders for hiring an underperforming

CEO, all decide entirely rationally but apparently somewhat perversely to pay over the odds. Something akin to Cohen's criticism of the difference principle applies here – unless conforming actions are mandated, that is, unless companies collectively recognise the need to tackle the problem of high executive pay, then the risk is that everyone regards it as somebody else's problem. What I have described as the standpoint question also comes into sharp focus – unless executives recognise that they have some responsibility for ensuring executive pay is moderated, in other words if they decide to leave it to their employers, then remuneration committees will continue to be caught in a dilemma that they cannot easily resolve.

Derek Parfit, the person referred to by G.A. Cohen in the head-note to this chapter, is sometimes regarded, along with John Rawls, as the other very great moral philosopher of the 20th century. Whereas Rawls spent a large part of his academic life at Harvard and produced one great work, *A Theory of Justice*, Parfit spend the whole of his academic career at Oxford and produced two great works: *Reasons and Persons*, in 1984, and *On What Matters*, in 2011, although it must also be said that *On What Matters* runs to two volumes and over thirteen hundred pages!

In *Reasons and Persons*, Parfit explains that we frequently face many-person prisoner's dilemmas, and that these are often at the root of our moral problems. Such dilemmas, he argues, have two kinds of solution, political or psychological, and the psychological solutions are, more often than not, ethical solutions. In his analysis, Parfit distinguishes between self-interested actions, S, and altruistic actions, A. In one of his earlier papers he explains this with the help of a decision tree, a version of which I have provided here as Figure 8.3. In the decision tree, X represents everyone involved in the decision, the members of the remuneration committee, the executives who are recipients of the awards, and so on.

Figure 8.3: Solutions to the remuneration committee's dilemma

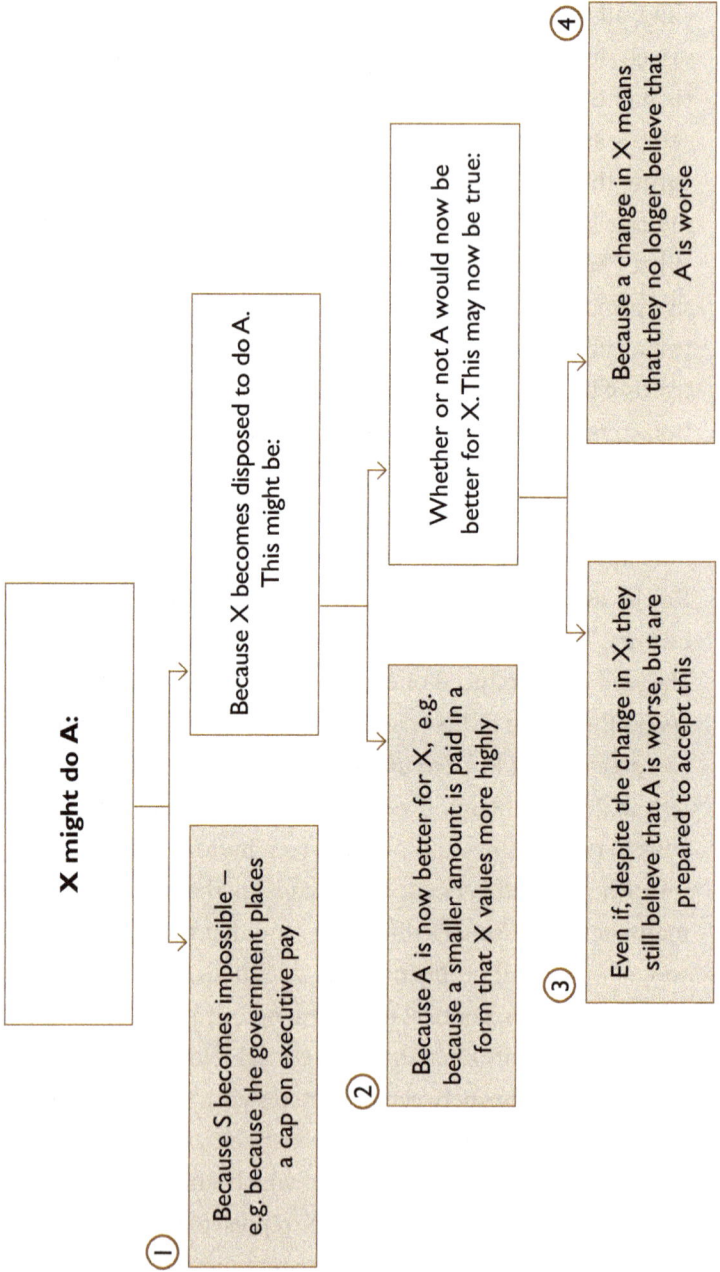

X might do A:

(1) Because S becomes impossible – e.g. because the government places a cap on executive pay

Because X becomes disposed to do A. This might be:

(2) Because A is now better for X, e.g. because a smaller amount is paid in a form that X values more highly

Whether or not A would now be better for X. This may now be true:

(4) Because a change in X means that they no longer believe that A is worse

(3) Even if, despite the change in X, they still believe that A is worse, but are prepared to accept this

In the case of the remuneration committee's dilemma, S (acting out of self-interest) means paying over the odds, and (if you are the executive who receives the payment) accepting the payment because everyone else is paying over the odds as well. A (acting altruistically) means paying more moderate remuneration, and accepting more moderate remuneration if you are the recipient, notwithstanding the actions of any other persons.

Parfit examines the circumstances in which X might do A. It might be because S becomes impossible – this is outcome (1) in the decision tree. This is a political solution – the government legislates to restrict high pay. Alternatively, X might become disposed to do A. This might be because of a change in circumstances that means that A leads to an outcome that is better for X than previously – for example, if all companies replaced their LTIPs with much smaller amounts paid in cash or in restricted stock, which executives value more highly than the LTIPs they have forgone – this is outcome (2). Alternatively, X might be disposed to do A whether or not it is better for them. This is one of the ethical solutions, outcome (3). X accepts the result even if it is worse for them, because they recognise that it is better for society as a whole. Indeed, the psychology of moral development means that it may no longer feel worse to X, because they have become disposed to the outcome which is better for society as a whole – namely, outcome (4), which is also an inherently ethical outcome.

In short, solving the remuneration committee's dilemma without external intervention requires more ethical behaviour to be exhibited by more people in business. I do not believe, as I know some do, that this is necessarily hard to achieve. Senior executives are motivated by far more than money: by the wish to succeed, by the need for achievement, by their own life's purpose. John Cryan, at the time newly recruited as the chief executive of Deutsche Bank, once said:

> I have no idea why I was offered a contract with a bonus in it because I promise you I will not work any harder or any less hard in any year, in any day because someone is going to pay me more or less.

Another chief executive once said, 'I have never believed that paying an additional £100,000, or £1 million or £10 million, makes anyone any more effective.' There is ample evidence to show that extrinsic rewards actually crowd out intrinsic motivation.[104]

When it comes to top executives, it might be better if businesses placed greater store on character and ethics rather than simply focusing on financial incentives, a theme that I will return to in the final chapter.

To sum up

Although executives are not in the main the greedy ethical egoists of popular culture, we have nevertheless seen, because of a flawed application of agency theory, a 'follow-the-leader' approach to the design of long-term incentive plans, and the 'leave-it-to-the-private-sector' policies of successive governments, unprecedented inflation in senior executive pay over the last 35 years. I have talked about two watershed events, the publication of the Norges Bank Investment Management's research paper on executive pay and the Weir Group's ditching of its LTIP, which I believe may have heralded a significant shift in 'normal science' when it comes to executive pay, and which may help to address the executive pay problem. In the next chapter, 'What is to be done?', I develop some policy proposals that may help to build on these foundations.

CHAPTER 9

What is to be done?

When presented with an apparently intractable problem, Lenin famously asked, 'What is to be done?', as I do here, given what I believe to be a significant ethical problem that is eating away at the roots of capitalism. But it is not my intention to foment a revolution.[105] Three things are required to make some progress: good government, ethical investors and responsible executives. I consider each of these in turn.

Good government

Good government in a liberal democracy, like good parenting, involves setting both boundaries and expectations. A wise parent takes great care when setting boundaries, selecting only those that are absolutely necessary and knowing when they are to be flexed or adapted. When it comes to pay, it is relatively straightforward

How to cite this book chapter:
Pepper, A. 2022. *If You're So Ethical, Why Are You So Highly Paid?: Ethics, Inequality and Executive Pay.* London: LSE Press. Pp. 111–129.
DOI: https://doi.org/10.31389/lsepress/eth License: CC BY-NC

for government to establish a lower boundary. Establishing an upper boundary is more problematic.

Sufficiency, the principle that all members of society should have an income that is sufficiently high to lead a dignified life, is a relevant factor for three of the four clusters of executives in the empirical study. Only in the case of free marketeers is sufficiency not a statistically significant ethical principle. Sufficiency implies a government should prescribe a lower boundary of a living minimum wage or some other kind of social safety net. Many countries have introduced a statutory minimum wage, although in most cases this is not set at a level that would qualify as a 'living wage', which is defined as the minimum income level necessary for a worker to meet their basic needs. A minimum wage differs from a living wage in that it may leave a worker still reliant upon government welfare programmes.

For welfare liberals, relational egalitarians and meritocrats, sufficiency is an ethical obligation at company level as well as for society as a whole. Executives who subscribe to the idea of sufficiency, particularly if applied at company level, would surely frown at the activities of 'gig economy' companies who seek to exploit the employed/self-employed worker boundary or use on-call or zero-hours contract workers in order to circumvent minimum wage regulations. They may also be critical of those who actively arbitrage differences in international labour markets by outsourcing work to countries with low wages and little employment protection. Unilever, the multinational consumer goods company, which describes itself as 'a global company with a global purpose', has made a living wage commitment – to pay a living wage to everyone who directly provides goods and services to Unilever – but it is still the exception, in this respect, rather than the rule.[106]

Establishing an upper boundary is more difficult. Sam Pizzigati has articulated the case for a maximum wage. He cites, for example, Felix Adler, a German philosopher, who in 1880 proposed a progressive income tax with a 100 per cent top rate 'when a certain high and abundant sum has been reached'. He also advocates what he calls 'the magic of maximum multiples', a cap on pay based on a multiples of average earnings.[107]

The one serious attempt to place an upper boundary on pay was Bill Clinton's 'million-dollar cap'. In his 1992 US presidential campaign manifesto, entitled 'Putting People First', Bill Clinton called for a strict cap on the tax deductibility of executive compensation. Companies would still be permitted to pay the CEOs and the next four most highly paid executive officers unlimited sums, but anything above $1 million would not be considered a reasonable business expense which would be allowable as a deduction for corporate tax purposes. Proponents of the policy argued that it would reduce 'excessive' compensation by raising the cost to the corporation. It appeared to be a serious attempt to place constraints on executive remuneration. However, after Clinton's election victory, his top economic advisers persuaded the president (overruling Labour Secretary Robert Reich) to qualify the proposals. 'Performance pay', including stock options and certain bonuses, would be exempt from the deductibility cap provided that it met certain criteria. Qualification for the exemption required advanced shareholder approval of a plan that linked compensation to specific objectively measurable performance targets, overseen by a compensation committee composed entirely of outside directors. Congress passed this proposal as part of a larger tax bill in 1993 and it became Section 162(m) of the Internal Revenue Code. In response, companies began limiting salaries to around $1 million and structuring the vast bulk of compensation as a reward for performance under a qualifying plan.

The impact of the million-dollar cap has been extensively investigated by labour economists and compensation consultants. The consensus conclusion is that the legislation has had relatively little real impact on overall compensation.[108] Anyone reviewing headline US CEO data over the last 25 years might regard this as self-evident. Recently, however, a surprising inclusion in the Tax Cuts and Jobs Act of 2017 modified Section 162(m) to remove the corporate tax deduction exemption for new compensation plans implemented after November 2017. At this point it is too early to say whether this change will have an effect on the overall level of top-executive pay.[109]

So what about setting expectations? At best it would seem that the position is confused. In 1998 Peter Mandelson, the British Labour Party politician who was at the time trade and industry secretary, assured a group of senior executives at Hewlett-Packard that the UK government was 'relaxed about people getting filthy rich, as long as they pay their taxes'. It was a statement he came to regret. In 2017, the Conservative prime minister Theresa May said that businesses who pay excessive salaries to senior executives represent the 'unacceptable face of capitalism' and were 'damaging the social fabric of our country'. But she was warned against plans to reform executive pay by introducing legally binding shareholder votes on compensation levels and abandoned a proposal to put workers on company boards.[110] In the US, Barack Obama was at one time a staunch critic of outsized pay packets, and, while the president placed a $500,000 salary cap on financial firms receiving government assistance after the 2008–2009 financial crisis, he also said of two Wall Street business leaders, 'I, like most Americans, don't begrudge people success of wealth

– that is part of the free-market system.' Donald Trump, perhaps unexpectedly, criticised excessive CEO pay when he said, 'It's disgraceful … you see these guys making enormous amounts of money, it's a total and complete joke', yet, while he was president, US CEO pay continued to increase rapidly while average employee wages remained largely unchanged. Notwithstanding changes to Section 162(m) of the tax code, referred to above, Trump's Tax Cuts and Jobs Act of 2017, the largest overhaul of the US tax regime in three decades, incorporated a regressive adjustment to taxes that predominantly favoured higher earners.[111]

What successive governments in the US and UK do appear to have been able to agree about, however, is the importance of transparency and in giving shareholders a 'say on pay'. The UK was the first country to introduce a non-binding vote on directors' pay in 2002 by providing shareholders with an advisory vote on the directors' remuneration report at the annual shareholders' meeting. Although not binding on the company, the impact of a substantial negative vote can be significant, as shareholder revolts against Vodafone, Royal & Sun Alliance and especially GlaxoSmithKline in 2003 have shown. In the US, equivalent say-on-pay provisions were introduced by the Dodd–Frank Wall Street Reform and Consumer Protection Act of 2010 as part of the overhaul of financial regulation following the 2008–2009 global financial crisis. The conclusion, 'leave it to shareholders', appears now to have been widely accepted by governments.

The other way governments can place constraints on high pay is by applying progressively higher rates of taxation on higher incomes. Robert Nozick, for example, has pointed out that redistributive tax would be required to maintain an egalitarian pattern of distribution in a society in which wages were not strictly controlled by the government. This is not the place for a detailed examination of the ethics and economics of progressive taxation, which are extraordinarily complex, other than to note in passing that:

- John Rawls argues that the tax and benefits system should be designed so as to maximise the net income of the worst-off members of society, and that this is justified on the basis that a fully equalising taxation system would undermine incentives for the more talented in such a way that everyone would end up being worse off.
- Harry Frankfurt believes that those below the sufficiency threshold should be net recipients under any tax and welfare system, but that redistributive taxation is unnecessary once everyone passes the threshold – when it comes to taxation over and above the poverty threshold, sufficientarians are largely indifferent.
- G.A. Cohen argues that a highly progressive taxation system is justified on egalitarian welfarist principles.
- Ronald Dworkin favours gift and inheritance taxes as a way of eliminating 'brute luck'.
- Joseph Heath favours taxes that rectify market imperfections, such as carbon and other environmental taxes that are designed to eliminate negative externalities.
- Robert Nozick famously argues that income tax breaches our right to self-ownership of our labour and is therefore tantamount to theft.

… none of which should be a surprise to anyone, given the views of the six philosophers which were set out earlier in the book.

It is also worth noting that, when asked in the 2020 British Social Attitudes Survey whether taxes in Britain for those with high incomes were much too high, about right or too low, less than a third of participants thought they were too high, around a third thought they were about right, and more than a third thought they were too low.[112] There would seem to be scope, in the UK at least, for higher marginal rates of tax on those with the highest incomes.

Ethical investors

Two words in common usage – 'good' and 'value' – have puzzled economists and philosophers alike for centuries. In economics, a 'good' is a noun meaning 'a thing of value' – *The Economist*'s *Dictionary of Economics* defines a good as 'any physical object, natural or manmade, or service rendered, that could command a price in a market'. In ethics, 'good' is a normative concept, meaning 'that which conforms to the moral ideal'; for example, Plato defines the good in his theory of forms as 'a perfect, eternal, and changeless entity existing outside space and time, in which particular good things share'. Other philosophers who do not subscribe to Plato's metaphysics might support the moral ideal of an 'absolute good' without agreeing that it has to be an existent object; for example, the Cambridge philosopher G.E. Moore believes that what is good is axiomatic, an unprovable rule or first principle accepted as true because it is self-evident or particularly useful. 'Good' can only be defined by extension, by listing examples of things that are good. It cannot be defined by intension, by specifying the necessary and sufficient conditions for something to be 'good'.

'Value' has caused almost as much debate in economics as 'good' has in ethics. In economics, 'value' means something of worth, and is sometimes further subdivided into either 'value in use', being the pleasure a commodity generates for its owner, or 'value in exchange', being the quantity of other commodities (or more usually money) which something can be exchanged for. In ethics, value(s), more often discussed in the plural, are basic and fundamental beliefs that guide or motivate attitudes or actions. Values help to determine what is important to us. They are personal qualities that we choose to embody to guide our actions.

For a long time, economists and philosophers have debated about 'good' and 'value' in their separate disciplinary silos. The arcane academic debates have rarely been of much interest to practitioners. Investors have a sense of what is and is not of 'value'. Craftsmen, teachers, parents, indeed all citizens have beliefs about what is and is not 'good', even if they do not always agree. More recently, however, academic debates at the interface of ethics and economics have become surprisingly real for investment professionals. 'ESG investing', which involves the consideration of environmental, social and governance factors alongside financial measures in the investment decision-making process, has gone mainstream. Over a quarter of total assets under management are now in socially responsible companies. Socially responsible investment management has grown into a $40 trillion industry. Two-thirds of global consumers are willing to spend more for products and services that are sustainable, and increasingly seek out goods with an 'ethically produced' certification.[113]

Investors – and I am thinking here specifically of institutional investors, the pension funds, banks, insurance companies and other financial services companies that dominate the stock market in the UK and the US – have one very important group of stakeholders – namely, us! – as contributors to pension funds, mutual funds and as citizens, if we are lucky enough to live in countries like Norway or Singapore with sovereign wealth funds. It has now been established beyond reasonable doubt in most jurisdictions that institutional investors are allowed to incorporate ESG

Figure 9.1: Key issues in ESG (governance) investing

Governance	
Corporate governance	Corporate behaviour
• Board diversity	• Business ethics
• **Executive pay**	• Anti-competitive practices
• Ownership and control	• Tax transparency
• Accounting	• Corruption and instability
	• Financial system instability

considerations into their investment analysis – although not all have decided to do so.[114] For example, the Law Commission in England and Wales has confirmed that pension fund trustees and others with fiduciary responsibilities are entitled to take ESG factors into account when making investment decisions.[115]

So far so good, but what has all this got to do with executive pay? MSCI is a global provider of stock markets indices and multi-asset portfolio analysis tools. They categorise key issues in ESG investing in a hierarchy with three primary headings, 10 secondary headings and – under the headings of corporate governance and corporate behaviour – nine tertiary headings. While under the environment heading MSCI identifies things like climate change and the preservation of natural resources, and under the social heading it includes the health and safety of human capital, international supply chain labour standards, product liability, chemical safety, privacy and data security, the governance heading is divided into corporate governance and corporate behaviour, with further subdivisions as shown in Figure 9.1. I have highlighted executive pay in bold.

Thus, company policies on executive pay are one of the things that ESG investors are required to take into account, albeit at a tertiary level of priority.

What about investment practices more generally? In 2010, in the aftermath of the global financial crisis, the Financial Reporting Council in the UK, the independent regulator which oversees the corporate governance code and financial reporting, published a 'stewardship code' for institutional investors. This helped to crystallise a view that institutional investors are part of the solution to the crisis in capitalism – that increased shareholder involvement in governance is essential to the development of sustainable long-term corporate value that is created in a way that is consistent with wider environmental and societal objectives. According to this view, institutional investors have an important role to play in holding boards of directors and senior business leaders to account. The stewardship code, which was updated in 2020, requires investors to publish annual stewardship reports that explain how they have shouldered their responsibilities. Many large investors now report on a global basis.

Legal & General Investment Management (LGIM) is one of Europe's largest asset managers, and one of the 10 largest in the world. It has been publishing an annual 'Active Ownership Report' for a decade, and in October 2020 issued a policy document setting out its principles on executive pay for the companies in which it invests. Its stewardship reports included a section on executive compensation, which in the 2020 report came under the heading 'Pay and Income Inequality'. It describes how LGIM has campaigned for companies to pay a living wage and increase pension contribution levels for employees. In 2020 there were 341 proposals to adopt new senior executive remuneration policies at UK companies, and in 128 cases LGIM voted against adoption.[116] Other large institutional investors, including Vanguard, Blackrock and Norges Bank Investment Management, are similarly actively engaging with the remuneration committees of portfolio

Figure 9.2: FTSE 100 CEO and other director total earnings, 2000–2020

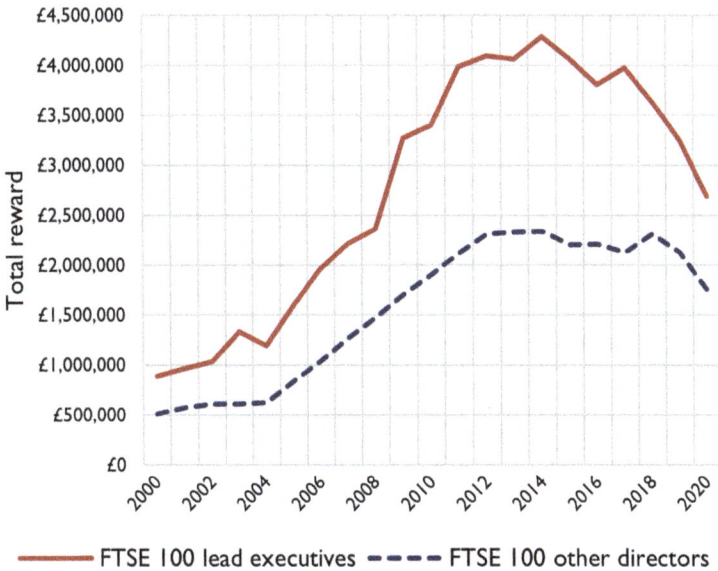

FTSE 100 lead executives   - - - - FTSE 100 other directors

companies on the subject of executive pay and are increasingly encouraging moderation as well as simplification in pay practices.

There are signs that investors' focus on executive compensation is having some effect, at least in the UK. Between 2000 and 2014, FTSE 100 CEO median total earnings increased from £885,000 to £4,285,000, an average annual increase of around 11 per cent – see Figure 9.2.[117] The median total pay of other directors increased at roughly the same rate, from £505,000 in 2000 to £2,340,000 in 2014. During the same period, private sector average earnings grew from £16,224 in 2000 to £24,232, an annualised increase of just over 2.7 per cent. For comparison, the annualised increase in the retail prices index over the same period was 2.8 per cent.

With the important proviso that correlation does not imply causation, you can see from the chart that after 2014, which is roughly the time that big institutional investors started to take a serious interest in the pay of executives in portfolio companies, something interesting happens – the curves flatten out and then start to decline. CEO pay actually fell from £4,065,000 in 2015 to £3,250,000 in 2019, the year before the start of the COVID–19 pandemic, when there was a sharp decline in executive pay. During the same period, average private sector earnings grew at just under 2.3 per cent per year, from £24,908 in 2015 to £27,872 in 2019. As a result, the ratio of CEO pay to average earnings reduced from 163:1 to 117:1 in 2019. In 2020, median FTSE 100 CEO pay was £2,690,000 and the ratio of CEO pay to average earnings fell to 95:1.

In the US, top pay rates have been flat for some time, but at very much higher levels than in the UK. Fortune 350 CEO pay increased rapidly from an average of $5,975,000 in 1995, peaking at $21,550,000 in 2000, declining to $16,045,000 in 2016 following the long recession after the global financial crisis, before levelling out at around $18 million in 2018. Pay ratios compared with typical workers are also much higher, increasing from 129:1 in 1995, peaking at 386:1 in 2000, and levelling out at 278:1 in 2018.[118]

But once again we must not get carried away and assume that investors have fixed the problem. Larry Fink, founder, chairman and CEO of Blackrock, whose annual letters to CEOs have increasingly focused on the importance of corporate purpose, stakeholders and long-term value creation in an environmentally and socially acceptable manner, in 2020 retained his position as the highest-paid chief executive in the asset management industry. The chiefs of 31 US and European asset management businesses took home pay and bonuses totalling $233 million in 2019, an average of around $7.5 million each. More concerningly, many big investment companies, including Vanguard, Fidelity, Capital Group and Wellington, do not publish data on senior staff pay. Such secrecy potentially undermines the idea that strengthening institutional investors' focus on ESG issues in response to pressures from retail investors may help to address the crisis in capitalism.[119]

Responsible executives

In considering 'what is to be done' at the level of the executive, we are forced back into the remuneration committee's dilemma – how can remuneration committees that determine what executives are paid be discouraged from participating in the economic game that inexorably leads to the ratcheting up of executive pay?

In searching for an answer, we first need to identify all the parties to the remuneration committee's dilemma. These are, first, the members of the remuneration committee of the company which employs the executive in question, say the CEO of Company X; second, the remuneration committees of all other companies, Y, Z etc., which are regarded as potentially competing for the services of the CEO of Company X; third, and critically, the CEO of Company X themselves. The fact that the CEO is also a player in the game adds a layer of complexity in comparison with a standard prisoner's dilemma: the remuneration committee of Company X must consider not just their own motivation (that is, wanting to ensure that their CEO is paid at least as well as the competition) but also what actually motivates the CEO.

When it comes to pay, our judgements, including those of highly paid executives, are framed by a strong sense of fairness, by a belief that there should be some correspondence between inputs and outputs, some proportionality between contribution and reward. This is known by economists as 'the fair wage–effort hypothesis' and explained by psychologists in terms of 'equity theory'. According to the fair wage–effort hypothesis, all workers proportionately withdraw effort if their actual wages fall short of a fair wage; conversely, if paid more than a fair wage (known by economists as 'efficiency wages'), the additional productivity of highly motivated workers will exceed the marginal cost of excess pay. This begs the question – what is a fair wage? Through their research on equity theory, psychologists have demonstrated that we determine what a fair wage is by making comparisons with the relative rewards received made by 'referent others', allowing for any differences in effort and ability – so the CEO of Company X might compare his or her reward with the pay of CEOs of Companies Y, Z etc., taking into account their perception of relative contributions. They will feel more motivated if they come out favourably in this comparison, and demotivated if they do not. To illustrate, consider the following.

> Jean is invited to join the senior management team of Company J with a total reward package worth £187,500. Jacques, a contemporary of Jean's with comparable expertise and experience, is invited to join the senior management team of Company Q with a total reward package of £195,000. Subsequently, Jean discovers that the average total reward package of her peers in Company J's management team is £180,000. Jacques discovers that the average total reward package of his peers in Company Q's management team is £202,500. All other things being equal, who do you think is likely to be more highly motivated? Possible answers: (A) Jean; (B) Jacques; (C) they are likely to be equally motivated.

In a survey of senior executives from around the world published in an academic journal, Jean, the executive receiving the lower absolute but higher relative amount, was chosen by 345 participants (45.6 per cent of the total sample). Jacques, the executive receiving the higher absolute sum, was chosen by 234 participants (31.0 per cent), with 177 participants (23.4 per cent) expressing the view that Jean and Jacques would be equally motivated. Comparable discrepancies between relative and absolute amounts have been reported in surveys of other workers. In short, the CEO's perception of what is fair, and therefore the remuneration committee's beliefs about what the CEO will perceive to be fair, become critical to the outcome of the remuneration committee's dilemma.

I now return to the ethical solutions to the remuneration committee's dilemma identified by Derek Parfit and described towards the end of Chapter 8. The dilemma can be solved if the remuneration committee has reason to believe that the executive in question would be prepared to accept an outcome even if, potentially, it was worse for them – that is, if ethical sentiments trump envy or greed.

Some of the most popular executive education programmes are about leadership. Consider the following: Oxford Education Leadership Programme over eight weeks, seven to 10 hours per week, from which you will 'walk away with tools and frameworks to refine your personal leadership purpose, in alignment with the purpose of your organisation'; the Stanford Executive Programme – 'be a leader who matters, leadership in extraordinary times, rediscover authenticity and renewed passion'; Harvard Business School's suite of executive leadership programmes, including 'authentic leader development', 'ascending the peak: finding the leader within', 'leadership for senior executives', and the 'women's leadership forum'; London Business School's numerous leadership programmes, including 'sustainability leadership and corporate responsibility' and 'leading businesses into the future'. I could go on. But the study of leadership is not a new phenomenon. Philosophers have been teaching and researching about leadership for centuries. They just call it something else – in particular, they talk about 'virtue ethics' and sometimes 'character'. Plato and Aristotle, to name but two, were fascinated by questions of character and virtue. Plato believed in absolutes – four 'cardinal virtues' – wisdom, temperance, courage and justice. Aristotle believed in the 'golden mean', and that virtues represent an equilibrium point between different tendencies. He was also very interested in how leaders find their individual life's purpose – their 'telos', in ancient Greek. To the ancients the study of ethics was the study of character, based on the principle that 'good (or virtuous) things are done by good (virtuous) people'. In medieval times and during the Enlightenment philosophers seemed to lose interest in the virtue ethics approach, and it was only at the beginning of the 20th century that it was rescued, first by Elizabeth Anscombe and Philippa Foot at Somerville College in Oxford, and later on by Alasdair MacIntyre with books such as *After Virtue*.[120] Studying character is back in fashion. One example is 'The Character Project' at Oxford University, the stated purpose of which is to address the question 'how do we best equip students to be the responsible values-based leaders that we need?'

It is in the work of Aristotle and his successors, along with Derek Parfit, that I believe we find the solution to the remuneration committee's dilemma. Aristotle believed in the importance of balance. He demonstrated that more is not always better; indeed at some point excessive competitiveness and ambition lead to jealousy and greed, even if too little results in apathy and indifference – see Figure 9.3.

Figure 9.3: Aristotle's conception of virtue

Competitiveness
Ambition
Motivation

Absence: ⟵————————————⟶ Excess:

Apathy   Jealousy
Indifference   Greed

⬆

The mean

Thus, with Aristotle in mind, we might conclude that too great a focus on the extrinsic motivation of senior executives through pay and rewards will crowd out intrinsic motivation, the pleasure and pride that come from a job well done, as well as contributing to inequality and societal discord.

John Kay, one of the leading business economists of his generation and a man I much admire, has talked more widely about the importance of balance in business. 'The scales fell from my eyes,' he once said, 'when I realised it was not the job of a company director to maximise anything. It was their job to balance.'[121] In *The Kay Review of UK Equity Markets and Long-Term Decision Making*, which was published in 2012, he wrote:

> We might ask why it is necessary or appropriate to pay bonuses to the directors of large companies at all. Many people doing responsible and demanding jobs – cabinet ministers, judges, surgeons, research scientists – do not receive bonuses, and would be insulted by the suggestion that the prospect of bonuses would encourage them to perform their duties more conscientiously. There are many criticisms of these professions, but rarely that they are not making the maximum effort. In all of these

activities, successful performance is inherently rewarding, and the prospect of such a reward provides effective
alignment of private and public interest.

The Kay Report concludes that companies should structure directors' remuneration so that incentives are related to sustainable
long-term business performance. Incentives should be provided
only in the form of company shares that are held until after the
executive has retired from the business. Investment managers
should be remunerated in a similar way.[122] There is much to be
recommended in this approach.

To sum up

In this chapter, in addressing the question 'what is to be done?' I
have set out what I believe to be the roles and responsibilities of
four parties – governments, companies, investors and executives
– in tackling the problem of inflation in top pay. In sum:

- Governments are ultimately responsible for ensuring
that there is distributive justice in society. They must set
the right moral tone (and, in this respect, be more like
Theresa May than Peter Mandelson), as well as appropriate policies on tax, disclosure and corporate governance. But it is clear that companies and executives are
not thereby absolved of their ethical responsibilities.

- Companies have a responsibility to pay executives proportionately, to pay other employees appropriately,
to provide all their workers with a living wage, and to
manage intra-firm inequality. It would help if remuneration committees recognised that highly leveraged stock
options and LTIPs with strong performance metrics are

largely ineffective. They should be replaced instead with simpler, more moderate pay arrangements, based around salaries, cash bonuses and perhaps restricted stock – for more details, see Chapter 8. At the same time, top executives should be required to build up substantial holdings in own company shares, to be held over the long term, in order to align their interests with those of shareholders.

- Investors have a responsibility to steward their assets properly. This includes ensuring the executives who run their portfolio companies do not extract economic rents in the form of excessive pay. For institutional investors it also means ensuring that they themselves do not extract excessive remuneration from the funds which they manage on behalf of pensioners and other retail investors.
- Executives must accept that there are ethical restrictions on their right to receive, and subsequently to retain, excessive income.

All these things may require further changes in the course of time to stewardship and corporate governance codes. They may require more government intervention to provide a catalyst for change. The issues I have outlined in this chapter also provide a justification, if one is needed, for the introduction of higher marginal tax rates to counter inequality and to provide additional financial support for the worst-off members of society.

The financialisation of business, which has been a feature of the UK and US economies over the last 30 years, has led to the current crisis in the general public's perception of the ethics of business and business leaders. This crisis will remain unsolved unless there is a greater focus on income inequality and the ethics of high pay.

CHAPTER 10

Afterword and postscript

I have tried to be dispassionate in setting out different theories and empirical viewpoints about senior executive reward. It is time to get off the fence. A question I am frequently asked, not unreasonably, is: what is my personal opinion about top pay? Perhaps there is a clue in the overall approach that I have taken in this book.

To explain, I must tell one further story. While hardly on all fours with Mark Twain's fable of *The Prince and the Pauper*, it is nevertheless a moral tale.[123] Between 2007, when direct line insurer Admiral Group plc joined the FTSE 100, and 2018, when Martin Sorrell, the chief executive of WPP, a global communications, advertising and public relations company, resigned after a board-level investigation into his personal conduct and use of company money, Sorrell and the CEO of Admiral (Henry Engelhardt, until

How to cite this book chapter:
Pepper, A. 2022. *If You're So Ethical, Why Are You So Highly Paid?: Ethics, Inequality and Executive Pay.* London: LSE Press. Pp. 131–138.
DOI: https://doi.org/10.31389/lsepress/eth License: CC BY-NC

he was succeeded by his business partner, David Stevens, in 2015) were regularly the highest- and lowest-paid lead executives in the FTSE 100, respectively. During this 12-year period Martin Sorrell was paid a total of £265 million, an average of £22 million per year. For the purposes of comparison, FTSE 100 CEOs were paid on average a total of £43 million between 2007 and 2018, around £3.6 million per year. In stark contrast, Engelhardt and Stevens were paid around £360,000 annually.

But we need to dig a little deeper. Between 2007 and 2018 Martin Sorrell's LTIPs paid out a total of £202 million, including a bumper payment of £63 million in 2015, when Sorrell's total earnings amounted to £70 million. Engelhardt and Stevens did not receive any LTIP payments. Admiral Group's annual directors' remuneration report explained the position like this:

> Henry Engelhardt and David Stevens are founding Directors. They and the Remuneration Committee continue to hold the view that the significant shareholdings held by them provide a sufficient alignment of their interest in the performance of the Group with the interests of other shareholders. In light of this, their remuneration packages consist only of a below market rate salary and benefits such as private medical cover, permanent health insurance and death in service cover. ... Henry Engelhardt and David Stevens have not participated, nor is it intended that they participate, in any Group share schemes. (Admiral Group plc Directors' Remuneration Report 2015)

Engelhardt and Stevens were major shareholders in Admiral. When dividends are taken into account, their average annual earnings amounted to around £22 million in total, more comparable with Martin Sorrell's total annual earnings (he also owned shares in WPP) of around £29 million.

Engelhardt and Stevens acquired their shares when they led the management buyout of Admiral from its parent company, Lloyd's managing agency Brockbank plc. Between 1999 and 2004, when Admiral was floated on the London Stock Exchange, its market capitalisation grew from £80 million to £711 million. The two business partners were entrepreneurs. The growth in the value of their shares represented a return, if you like, on their 'entrepreneurial capital' (their capabilities as founders, innovators, and growers of new business). The dividends they received on their shares after flotation was a return on their financial capital. Their earnings from employment were a return on their human capital.

Martin Sorrell was also an entrepreneur. In 1985 he invested $325,000 in WPP when it was a shell company called Wire and Plastic Products, worth $1.3m. Through a series of acquisitions, notably of J. Walter Thompson in 1987 and Ogilvy & Mather in 1989, he built WPP into a global advertising powerhouse. He amassed great wealth as a result – in 2020, at the time of his divorce from his second wife, his net worth was reported to be £368 million.

It is in this context, having compared the approaches taken to long-term incentives by the remuneration committees of WPP and Admiral, Sorrell's average annual pay from WPP of £22 million between 2007 and 2018 in comparison with the FTSE 100 CEO average of £3.6 million, and taking into account the fact that Mark Read, Sorrell's successor at WPP, was paid £2.6 million in 2019, it is hard not to conclude that Martin Sorrell was extracting large economic rents from the shareholders of WPP. More than anything else, for reasons which I have already explained, it is economic rents that represent the most troubling aspect of executive pay. Liberal democracies need entrepreneurs if they are to thrive economically, and financial capital has a right to receive a reasonable economic return – as does human capital: the ability, education and experience that we accumulate over time and apply in return for wages, if we are employees, or for other sources of income if we are self-employed. What is not justified is the extraction of rents, payments made to a factor of production (land, labour or capital) in excess of that which is necessary to bring that factor into production.

Engelhardt and Stevens received considerable returns to their entrepreneurship, amassing substantial shareholdings in the company for which they continued to work. They were subsequently content to receive the major portion of their income in the form of dividends. Their interests were firmly aligned with those of other shareholders precisely because they were also shareholders. Their more modest employment income was similarly much more closely aligned with that of other employees.

Martin Sorrell, on the other hand, appeared to want the penny and the bun. He is thus, in a sense, an example of 'the exception that proves the rule'. The thesis of this book is that senior executives are not typically ethical egoists who use their power in the corporate hierarchy to extract rents in the form of very high pay, although perhaps Martin Sorrell is one of the exceptions.[124]

Karl Popper famously chose the statement 'all swans are white' as an example of the problem with general laws. For nearly 1,500 years after its first use in the 2nd century AD a metaphor by the Roman poet Juvenal, the black swan existed in the Western imagination to represent something that could not exist. This was until Dutch explorers became the first Europeans to see black swans in Western Australia towards the end of the 17th century. At the last count there were between 1.5 and 1.6 million swans in the world, of which around 15 per cent were black or black-necked. This means that 'most swans are white' is a reasonable rule of thumb, especially in North and South America, Europe and Africa.[125]

In the same way I believe that it is perfectly reasonable to say 'most business executives are not bad people'. Nevertheless, the occasional behaviours of a minority are indicative of personal greed.

In the previous chapter I explored the question that logically follows from this rough and ready rule – 'if executives are so ethical, why are they so highly paid?' The research I have described in this book has shown that business executives are 'welfare liberals', 'relational egalitarians', 'meritocrats' or 'free marketeers'. They are not, generally speaking, ethical egoists who believe that moral agents are entitled to act in their own self-interest. Do not assume that all top executives are greedy people who are on the make – some are, but most are not. They have, however, been the most fortunate beneficiaries of a system that has been running hot for too long.

There is no ethical justification for paying economic rents in the form of excessive remuneration. Executives and investors, along with governments and major institutions, all share a moral responsibility for ensuring that there is distributive justice in society. But the problem of high pay will not be solved by technical means alone – the various parties involved must also recognise their ethical obligations. When it comes to top pay, for too long companies have behaved as if they are in the equivalent of an arm's race. It is a mad, bad system, and it needs to change if inflation in executive pay is to be brought under control.

I am generally sceptical about the use of sporting metaphors in business. Nevertheless, I want to conclude with a story about Graham Henry, the Auckland schoolteacher who became coach of the New Zealand rugby union team, the legendary All Blacks.[126] In 2004, when Henry was appointed coach, the All Blacks were in disarray. They had lost in the semi-finals of the Rugby World Cup in 2003 and finished bottom in the Tri Nations tournament the following year, failures that were accompanied by reports of low morale and ill-discipline. Over seven years, and after overcoming the major disappointment of being knocked out by France in a close game in the quarter-finals of the 2007 World Cup, Henry built the All Blacks into a team that became known as the greatest sports team of all time, winning 88 times in 103 test matches, including an emphatic series win over the British and Irish Lions in 2005, five Tri Nations tournaments, and eventually winning the World Cup in 2011. Graham Henry's mantra, arrived at after serious self-reflection by the team, was this: 'Better people make better All Blacks.'

My personal belief is that more responsible executives – those who focus on the good as well as goods, on values as well as creating value, and on distributive justice as well as personal reward – make better businesspeople too.

Postscript – Mrs Taylor's pirates

I began this book with the story of Mrs Taylor's pirate band and her claim, as captain, to have prior rights over one-half of any treasure.

Curiously, quite a lot is known about the organisation and economics of piracy in the 17th and 18th centuries, and the retention of so sizeable a share of the pirates' booty by the captain would in fact have been most unusual.[127] Pirate ships have been described by one historian as 'sea-going stock companies' in which each member of the pirate crew held a share. As the pirate ships would typically have been seized or stolen in the first place, they were in effect in common ownership. The captain was democratically elected by the crew for his skills as a seaman and plunderer. To maintain the balance of power, a quartermaster, with power to allocate provisions, distribute loot and adjudicate among crew members, was separately elected to look after the crew's interests. Both appointments could be overturned – pirate crews could vote the captain and quartermaster out of office for any one of a number of specified reasons set out in the vessel's written constitution.

Plunder obtained during successful piratical activity would be divided into lots, with the first share allocated to cover necessary capital costs such as repairs to the ship. The second share would be used to compensate those who had lost limbs or suffered other injuries while fighting (for example, 600 pieces of eight was at one time the going rate for the loss of a right arm, 500 pieces of eight for the loss of the left arm, and so on).[128] Thereafter, among an average crew of 80 or more seafarers, the captain might draw four or five times one man's portion from the residual profits and the quartermaster might get an amount equal to two men's shares, while the rest of the crew participated equally, with boys getting half a man's portion. To avoid argument, any hard-to-value items of booty would be auctioned or sold and the cash proceeds distributed instead. No measurement problems here.

According to some historians, pirate ships were often more orderly, peaceful and well organised than many equivalent naval or merchant ships, which operated as autocracies under the iron hand of the captain, whose dictatorial rule was underpinned by maritime law. Merchant ships were typically owned by landlubbing investors, who would appoint seagoing captains to look after their interests, awarding them small shares in the vessels under their command. Captains thus had a partial claim over the residual profits of the ships they controlled – in this way, it was hoped, their interests would be aligned with those of the absent owners. On board a merchant ship the captain presided over a hierarchical organisation structure, retaining absolute power over resources, payments, manpower assignment and discipline. Regular sailors, at the bottom of the hierarchy, who typically came from the lowest ranks of society, drew fixed minimum wages and worked in appalling conditions. While this system of 'merchant ship autocracy' was often efficient, merchant ships were rarely happy places.

Lest we get too carried away with the positive aspects of piratical society, such as democracy, separation of powers, written constitutions and fair shares, we should also remember the undercurrent of violence, racial discrimination and gender inequality that no doubt underpinned the society of these 'nests of rogues', as Governor William Spotswood of New Providence in the Bahamas once described them. Beyond the confines of the ship, pirates were no respecters of life or property rights and they lived their lives well outside the reach of law for as long as they could.

Nevertheless, it is interesting to note that, within the boundaries of piratical society, these buccaneers appear to have behaved like 'relational egalitarians'. But then perhaps, harking back to Ronald Dworkin's thought experiment about shipwrecked sailors which I described in Chapter 5, the Oxford philosopher would not have been particularly surprised by this!

Appendix: Background survey research for this book

The intellectual roots of the research method that lies behind this book can be found in experimental philosophy – an emerging, but contested, field of philosophical enquiry. Experimental philosophers make use of empirical data – gathered, for example, by surveys, to inform debate on fundamental philosophical questions. Some analytical philosophers oppose this type of enquiry, preferring instead a more traditional approach that relies on a priori justification and deductive reasoning. Proponents of experimental philosophy believe that probing the intuitions of ordinary people and subjecting the results to rigorous conceptual analysis is a perfectly valid, and indeed very robust, method of enquiry. They argue that this approach has particular validity when it comes to ethics.[129]

Most of the research described in this book was carried out between 2016 and 2020, working together with Dr Susanne Burri and Dr Daniela Lup, and supported by PwC. Data for the study were collected on our behalf by a market research company using an online survey instrument that we had designed. It was then handed to us, anonymised, in raw form for cleaning and analysis.

Methodology

Data collection was based on a list of pre-selection criteria (job title, earnings, industry sector, company size, nationality and country of residence), with a view to ensuring that only 'senior business executives' as defined for the purposes of the study were included in the sample. A panel-screener questionnaire was used to ensure that respondents who did not meet the pre-selection criteria were selected out. Quotas were agreed in advance to ensure that the sample was broadly representative of different ages, genders, industry sectors and nationalities. While data based on quota sampling cannot necessarily be guaranteed to be representative of the underlying population, the sample was quite large (n = 1,123) and well diversified, allowing for meaningful analysis. There is some justification for using quota sampling given that high-level business executives are notoriously difficult to access. Demographic and economic background information about respondents is given in Figures A.1, A.2, A.3 and A.4.

Figure A.1: The gender and age of respondents

Gender	Number	Per cent (%)
Male	721	64.2
Female	342	30.5
Not disclosed	60	5.3
Age		
Under 35	247	22.0
35–39	232	20.7
40–44	138	12.3
45–49	161	14.3
50–54	122	10.9
55–59	89	7.9
60–64	57	5.1
65 and over	23	2.1
Not disclosed	54	4.8

Figure A.2: The companies, job titles and salaries of respondents

Company ownership	Number	Per cent (%)
Listed public company	486	43.3
Private limited company	440	39.2
State-owned enterprise	85	7.6
Other	112	10.0
Job title		
CEO/president/MD	94	8.4
Other C-level executive	154	13.7
SVP/VP/director	875	77.9
Indicative total earnings		
$125,000–$149,000	389	34.6
$150,000–$349,000	317	28.2
$350,000–$724,999	141	12.6
$725,000–$999,999	58	5.2
≥ $1,000,000	68	6.1
Not disclosed	150	13.4

Figure A.3: The industry sector of respondents

Industry sector	Number	Per cent (%)
Technology	176	15.7
Business services	76	6.8
Financial services	76	6.8
Retail and consumer	69	6.1
Industrial manufacturing	64	5.7
Engineering and construction	63	5.6
Banking and capital markets	61	5.4
Government and public sector	55	4.9
Healthcare	48	4.3
Energy, utilities, mining	45	4.0
Transport and logistics	44	3.9
Pharmaceuticals	38	3.4
Automotive	28	2.5
Communications	28	2.5
Insurance	24	2.1
Chemicals	21	1.9
Asset management	16	1.4
Entertainment and media	16	1.4
Hospitality and leisure	16	1.4
Oil and gas	12	1.1
Defence	11	1.0
Capital and infrastructure	8	0.7
Metals	8	0.7
Forestry, paper and packaging	7	0.6
Aerospace	3	0.3
All others	110	9.8

Figure A.4: The country of respondents

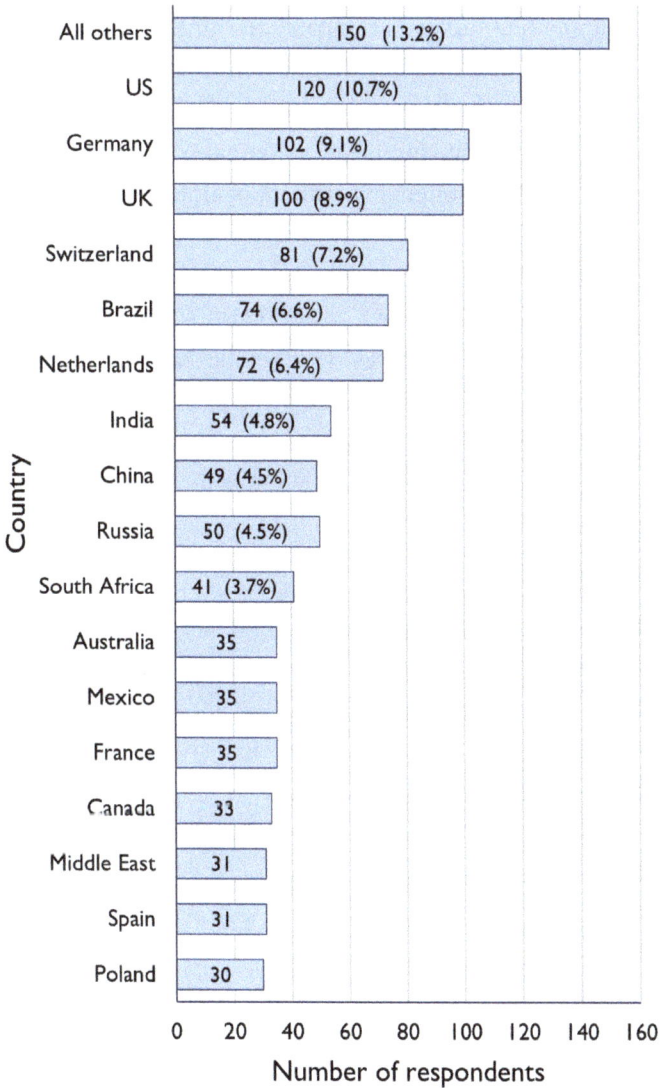

Note: The numbers in brackets in the top bars show the percentage of respondents from that country.

The thought experiment

To encourage our survey participants to think impartially about questions of distributive justice, we asked them to engage in a thought experiment that resembled John Rawls's 'original position', before answering the questionnaire. A fuller explanation of the way the thought experiment operated can be found in Chapter 3.

The questionnaire centred on the six principles of distributive justice described in Chapter 3 – see Figure 3.1 for more details. For each of the six principles, we provided a key claim and a rationale in order to introduce the principles to the survey participants. The six principles were assigned a random order and given neutral labels such as 'Principle A' or 'Principle B'. For each principle, we asked the respondents to what extent they agreed with each of the following three statements:

1. 'I would want an imaginary society that I might have to find my place in to be governed in accordance with this principle.'
2. 'A society governed by this principle would be a just society.'
3. 'The society that I currently live in is governed by this principle.'

Participants were given the option to 'strongly agree', 'agree', 'neither agree nor disagree', 'disagree' or 'strongly disagree' with the different statements. We coded participants' level of agreement as '+1' (strongly agree with a principle), '+0.5' (agree with the principle), '0' (neither agree nor disagree), '–0.5' (disagree) and '–1' (strongly disagree). Thus, the higher the average for a principle, the more agreement exists among the respondents that the principle expresses a distributive justice ideal.

In the second part of the questionnaire, we proceeded in a similar way, but asked participants to what extent they endorsed the different principles of justice as governing the distribution of income at company, rather than society, level. The order in which the different principles were presented was altered in the second part of the questionnaire to mitigate order effects. We also changed the terminology from 'principles' to 'statements' to make pairings between the first and second parts of the questionnaire less obvious.

In the third part of the survey, participants were invited to respond to a number of propositions such as 'corporations should take into account principles of fairness and distributive justice when determining their pay strategies' and 'questions of distributive justice should be settled exclusively at the level of society as a whole rather than also at the level of individual corporations'. In this way, and by asking other questions about justice principles at both society and company level, we were able to determine to what extent participants believed that matters of distributive justice were the responsibility of companies as well as governments. Participants were also given the opportunity to add additional unprompted narrative comments if they so wished. Some of these have been quoted in the opening sections for chapters detailing the different clusters (Chapters 4 to 7).

Some main findings

One of the main findings of our research was that there was a very pronounced pluralism of views about distributive justice. Our respondents showed agreement with multiple principles. The overt pluralism in participants' views on distributive justice indicated that business executives are drawn to rather complex

Figure A.5: How respondents were distributed across four clusters

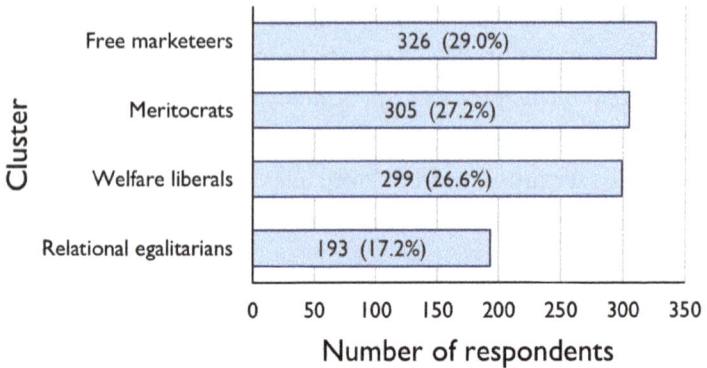

Note: *The numbers in brackets show the percentage of all respondents.*

conceptualisations of distributive justice. They appear to believe that distributive justice is governed by many different considerations that are not easily distilled into a single instructive formula. Another significant finding was that the majority of participants believed companies had as much responsibility for ensuring that there is distributive justice as governments or society as a whole.

To understand the plurality in respondents' views in more detail, we asked participants to rank-order their preferences – we then performed a cluster analysis on the ranked data. Cluster analysis involves partitioning data with the aim of uncovering groups ('clusters') of homogeneous observations. To determine the clusters, we used an algorithm that iteratively calculated cluster means. Multiple passes were made through the dataset, allowing observations to change group based on their distance from the recomputed mean. The algorithm stops when no further observations change cluster. Figure A.5 shows how many of our respondents were assigned to the different clusters. The results of the cluster analysis are shown in Figure A.6.

Figure A.6: Cluster analysis scores for the principles in each cluster

Cluster name	n	Principle					
		Equality of opportunity	Desert	Sufficiency	Maximin	Efficiency	Entitlement
Relational egalitarians	193	2.27	5.18	2.45	3.15	3.53	4.42
Meritocrats	305	2.02	2.19	2.12	5.13	4.23	5.30
Welfare liberals	299	5.27	1.89	2.44	3.02	4.12	4.25
Free marketeers	326	2.04	1.96	4.71	5.23	2.66	4.40

Notes: The numbers in each cell show the cluster analysis score for that principle in that cluster, correct to two decimal places. The intuitive meaning is that the lower the number, the higher the respondents valued a particular principle. Orange-shaded italic scores are statistically significant at p < 0.1 (a 10% level), meaning that the principle in question is associated with that cluster.

The first cluster here is a group of respondents that we labelled as 'relational egalitarians'. It is characterised by a relatively high level of endorsement of both equality of opportunity and sufficiency principles (detailed further in Chapter 5). The second cluster in Figure A.6, who we called 'meritocrats', is characterised by a relatively high preference for desert principles, as well as for equality of opportunity and sufficiency (Chapter 6). The third cluster, labelled 'welfare liberals', have a relatively high level of endorsement of the two needs-based principles, sufficiency and maximin, in addition to a high preference for desert (Chapter 4). The final cluster in Figure A.6, labelled 'free marketeers', emphasised desert, economic efficiency, and equality of opportunity principles (Chapter 7). Interestingly, entitlement did not feature significantly in any of the clusters. The bottom three clusters in Figure A.6 are broadly of equal size in our sample, but the relational egalitarians cluster is smaller than the other three.

We also investigated the extent to which the distribution of socio-demographic characteristics varied across clusters. Specifically, we calculated chi-squares to compare the observed age, gender, income, nationality, industry sector and type of company for each cluster with the expected data for the whole sample – see Figure A.7.

Some heterogeneity in distributive justice views is apparent in the data, but there are relatively few statistically significant differences in views of cluster members across such key demographic markers such as age, gender, income, nationality, company type or industry sector. Although the views of a free marketeer differ markedly from the views of (say) a welfare liberal, roughly equal numbers of free marketeers and welfare liberals occur among different age groups, income brackets, genders, industry sectors, etc.

Figure A.7: Comparing cluster demographics using chi-square scores

Cluster	Gender		Age		Nationality		Income		Industry		Ownership	
	χ^2	df	χ^2	df	χ^2	df	χ^2	df	χ^2	df	χ^2	df
Relational egalitarians	3.1	2	7.2	6	17.7	6	5.4	5	18.6	25	4.9	3
Meritocrats	1.0	2	**28.1**	6	18	16	9.6	5	18.4	25	1.6	3
Welfare liberals	1.2	2	**44.1**	6	**47.4**	16	**36.6**	5	*35.0*	25	2.0	3
Free marketeers	3.2	2	8.4	6	**47.6**	16	5.0	5	20.3	25	2.1	3

Notes: χ^2 denotes the chi-square score; df the associated degrees of freedom. Chi-square scores are designed to identify statistically unlikely patterns of association. The higher the score is (given the accompanying degrees of freedom), the less likely an association is to have arisen from random chance. Green shaded bold scores are statistically significant at $p < 0.01$ (the 1% level). Orange-shaded italic scores are statistically significant at $p < 0.1$ (the 10% level). White cells show scores that could have arisen through random chance (given the associated degrees of freedom).

However, we did note that among welfare liberals there are a disproportionally large number of Chinese nationals – 60 per cent of Chinese participants are characterised as welfare liberals; conversely, only 10 per cent of this cluster were Swiss nationals. The ages of welfare liberals are also interesting. They are relatively young – 33 per cent are under 35 years of age, with a further 30 per cent aged between 35 and 40. They also have comparatively lower incomes on average, in part perhaps because of their relatively younger age. Welfare liberals are also highly represented in the technology sector. The flipside of the high number of Chinese nationals who are welfare liberals is that only a small number (less than 10 per cent) of them are free marketeers. The age profile of meritocrats is skewed towards older executives – this cluster was under-represented in executives below the age of 40.

Further information

To learn more about this research and read a more detailed explanation of the methodology and a comprehensive discussion of the findings, please see:

Burri, Susanne, Lup, Daniela, and Pepper, Alexander. (2021) 'What do business executives think about distributive justice?' *Journal of Business Ethics*, 174(1), 15–33, https://doi.org/10.1007/s10551-020-04627-w. Licence: CC BY 4.0.

Notes

1 Piketty, T. (2014) *Capital in the Twenty-First Century*. The Belknap Press of Harvard University Press, 315–21.

2 Press release, High Pay Centre: 'High Pay Day 2022: CEO pay for 2022 surpassed the earnings of the median UK full time worker just prior to 9am today', 7 January 2022. See also https://perma.cc/9RD5-RY5V

3 Press releases 4 January 2018, 15 August 2018, adamsmith.org; see also wired-gov net 'Adam Smith Institute – falling pay gap between CEOs and their employees is nothing to celebrate', 11 January 2022, https://perma.cc/TX7K-8Y9Z Peter Yeung, 'Why CEOs make so much money', 27 January 2021, https://perma.cc/D5BQ-LJK8

4 The Investment Association, press release, 19 November 2021, https://perma.cc/5GZU-HJNW

5 Justin Welby, quoted by George Parker, political editor, in the *Financial Times*, 8 September 2018, https://perma.cc/U4P2-CQGN

[6] Burri, S., Lup, D. and Pepper, A. (2021) 'What do business executives think about distributive justice?'. *Journal of Business Ethics*, 174(1), 15–33,
https://doi.org/10.1007/s10551-020-04627-w

[7] Dewey, J., and Tufts, J. (1908) *Ethics*. New York: Henry Holt and Company, 4–5.

[8] Piketty (2014) *Capital in the Twenty-First Century*, 1.

[9] Inequality data was downloaded in January 2021 from the World Inequality Database, https://wid.world/data

[10] Mark Twain's book *The Gilded Age: A Tale of Today* was co-authored by Charles Dudley Warner and published in 1873. The American sociologist Lewis Mumford is one of a number of scholars who wrote disparagingly about the enormous disparity of wealth between the richest and poorest members of society during the Gilded Age.

[11] The full title of Simon Heffer's book is *The Age of Decadence: Britain 1880 to 1914*. It was published in 2017 by Random House Books.

[12] Hobsbawm, E. (1987) *The Age of Empire, 1875–1914*. London: Weidenfeld & Nicolson, 46–48.

[13] Not everyone agrees with this description. For both sides of the argument see Wortel-London, D., and Cothran, B. (2020) 'A second gilded age? The promise and perils of an analogy', *The Journal of the Gilded Age and Progressive Era*, 19(2), 191–96, along with other articles in this special issue of the journal.

[14] Friedman, M. (1970) 'The social responsibility of business is to increase its profits', *New York Times Magazine*, 13 September.

[15] Jensen, M., and Meckling, W. (1976) 'Theory of the firm: Managerial behavior, agency costs and ownership structure'. *Journal of Financial Economics*, 3(4), 310,
https://doi.org/10.1016/0304-405X(76)90026-X

[16] See Krippner, G. (2005) 'The financialization of the American economy'. *Socio-Economic Review* 3, 173–208, https://doi.org/10.1093/SER/mwi008 and Krippner, G. (2011) *Capitalizing on Crisis: The Political Origins of the Rise of Finance*. Cambridge, MA: Harvard University Press; Davis, G.F.

(2009) *Managed by the Markets – How Finance Re-Shaped America*. Oxford University Press, 63. 'Lean, mean, and focused on its core competencies' is a quote from an essay by Jerry Davis entitled 'Corporate purpose needs democracy', published in the *Journal of Management Studies* in 2020. https://doi.org/10.1111/joms.12659

[17] Solow, R. (2017) 'Thomas Piketty is right', Chapter 2 of *After Piketty – The Agenda for Economics and Inequality* (eds Boushey, Delong and Steinbaum). Harvard University Press.

[18] US data in this section are from Mishel, L., and Kandra, J. (2020) 'CEO Compensation surged 14% in 2019 to $21.3 million'. Economic Policy Institute Report, epi/204513. UK data are drawn from a number of sources, including Income Data Services (for periods between 2000 and 2015), CIPD executive pay reports (for periods after 2015) and the Office for National Statistics Annual Survey of Hours and Earnings (all years). UK CEO pay data for period prior to 2000 was extrapolated from a number of different sources, including Conyon, M., Gregg, P., and Machin, S. (1995) 'Taking care of business: Executive compensation in the United Kingdom'. *The Economic Journal*, 105(430), 704–14, https://doi.org/10.2307/2235029 Cosh, A. (1975) 'The remuneration of chief executives in the United Kingdom'. *The Economic Journal*, 85(337), 75–94, https://doi.org/10.2307/2230529

[19] For CEO pay data in Germany, see Beck, D., Friedl, G., and Schäfer, P. (2020) 'Executive compensation in Germany', *Journal of Business Economics*, 90, 787–824, https://doi.org/10.1007/s11573-020-00978-y For all-employee pay data see the Federal Statistical Office Statistisches Bundesamt website. For pay ratios for France and Germany see Kotnik, P., Sakinç, M., and Guduraš, D. (2018) 'Executive compensation in Europe: Realized gains from stock-based pay' *Institute for New Economic Thinking*, Working Paper No. 78, 13 July 2018, https://perma.cc/BFJ8-9X2S

[20] Leijonhufvud, A. (1973) 'Life among the Econ'. *Western Economic Journal*, 11(3), 327–37,

https://doi.org/10.1111/j.1465-7295.1973.tb01065.x An article by the *FT*'s Gillian Tett reminded me about this article and confirmed how its message continues to be entirely relevant. Tett, G. (2021) 'When economic tribes go to war', *Financial Times*, 20 May, https://perma.cc/ULX7-BTR8

21 See, for example, Kamm, F. (2016) *The Trolley Problem Mysteries. The Berkeley Tanner Lectures*. New York: Oxford University Press. The trolley problem was first set out by Philippa Foot in 1967 in an essay entitled 'The problem of abortion and the doctrine of double effect'. This essay can be found in Foot, P. (1978) *Virtues and Vices and Other Essays in Moral Philosophy*. Oxford: Blackwell, 19–32.

22 See, for example, Toulmin, S. (1950) *The Place of Reason in Ethics*. Cambridge: Cambridge University Press.

23 Rawls, J. (1971) *A Theory of Justice*. Cambridge, MA: The Belknap Press of Harvard University Press, 12. Rawls's 'original position' plays a similar role to 'the state of nature' in the traditional social contract theories of Thomas Hobbes and Jean-Jacques Rousseau.

24 Misak, C. (2013) *The American Pragmatists*. Oxford University Press. Part II, Chapter 7, 'John Dewey', 133.

25 I much simplify here a philosophical debate about whether ethical facts exist or not; if so, whether they can be learnt through scientific processes (naturalism) or not (non-naturalism); if not, whether they are expressions of an attitude (expressionism) or are otherwise meaningless. In technical terms, I am assuming 'metaethical realism' – that is, ethical facts do exist. In pragmatic terms I am assuming that there is such a thing as ethical knowledge.

26 Miller, D. (1999) *Principles of Social Justice*. Cambridge, MA. Harvard University Press, 51. I am particularly indebted to David Miller's book for many of the arguments in this section.

27 The philosopher Alasdair MacIntyre distinguishes between what he calls 'internal goods', excellent products or perfect practice – for example, analytical skill or competitive intensity, which are desired in pursuit of our 'telos' (life's purpose), leading, if achieved, to 'eudamonia' (flourishing) – and 'external

goods', such as money, status or power, which may potentially distract from life's purpose if pursued for their own sake. See MacIntyre, A. (1981) *After Virtue – A Study in Moral Theory.* University of Notre Dame Press.

[28] Jensen and Meckling's seminal article is entitled 'Theory of the firm: Managerial behavior, agency costs and ownership structure'. It was published in 1976 in the *Journal of Financial Economics*, 3(4), 305–60, https://doi.org/10.1016/0304-405X(76)90026-X For tournament theory see Lazear, E., and Rosen, S. (1981) 'Rank-order tournaments as optimal labor contracts'. *Journal of Political Economy*, 89(5), 841–64, https://doi.org/10.1086/261010 For a review of optimal contracting theory see Edmans, A., and Gabaix, X. (2016) 'Executive compensation: A modern primer'. *Journal of Economic Literature*, 5(4), 1232–87, https://doi.org/10.1257/jel.20161153

[29] Jensen, M., and Murphy, K. (1990) 'Performance pay and top-management incentives'. *Journal of Political Economy*, 98(2), 225–64, https://doi.org/10.1086/261677 When Jensen and Murphy failed to find a strong empirical connection between CEO pay and performance, they argued that this was the result of political forces at the heart of the corporation and that companies should provide a greater proportion of total compensation in the form of incentive pay, thus switching from a positive to a normative line of argument – see Jensen, M., and Murphy, K. (1990) 'CEO incentives: it's not how much you pay, but how'. *Harvard Business Review,* 68(3), 138–53, https://perma.cc/9JJW-CKHM – I call this the 'J&M-twist'. Paul Samuelson (1963) described Milton Friedman's thesis that the truth of the assumptions is irrelevant to the acceptability of a theory, provided that the theory's predictions succeed, as the 'F-twist' – Samuelson, P. (1963) 'Problems of methodology – discussion'. *American Economic Review, Papers and Proceedings*, 53, 231–36. Steve Keen argues that Tony Lawson provides the 'L-correction' to the 'F-twist' by forcing economics to consider its ontology – see Lawson, T. (2015) *Essays on the Nature and State of Modern Economics.*

Abingdon: Routledge. Postface and Chapter 3. In the same spirit, I propose a 'P-correction' to Jensen's 'J&M-twist'.

[30] Tosi, H., Werner, S., Katz, J., and Gomez-Mejia, L. (2000) 'How much does performance matter? A meta-analysis of CEO pay studies'. *Journal of Management*, 26(2), 301–39, https://doi.org/10.1177/014920630002600207 Two subsequent meta-analytic reviews have continued to provide evidence that CEO pay and financial performance are not closely related: see van Essen, M., Otten, J., and Carberry, E. (2015) 'Assessing managerial power theory: A meta-analytic approach to understanding the determinants of CEO compensation'. *Journal of Management*, 26(2), 164–202, https://doi.org/10.1177/0149206311429378 and Aguinis, H., Gomez-Mejia, L., Martin, G., and Joo, H. (2018) 'CEO pay is indeed decoupled from CEO performance: Charting a path for the future'. *Management Research*, 16(1), 117–36, https://doi.org/10.1108/MRJIAM-12-2017-0793

[31] See Gabaix, X., and Landier, A. (2008) 'Why has executive pay increased so much?' *Quarterly Journal of Economics*, 123(1), 49–100, https://doi.org/10.1162/qjec.2008.123.1.49 Edmans, A., and Gabaix, X. (2016) 'Executive compensation: A modern primer'. *Journal of Economic Literature*, 54(4), 1232–87, https://doi.org/10.1257/jel.20161153 Baker, G., Jensen, M., and Murphy, K. (1988) 'Compensation and incentives: Practice vs.theory'. *Journal of Finance*, 43(3), 609, https://doi.org/10.1111/j.1540-6261.1988.tb04593.x

[32] See Bebchuk, L., Fried, J., and Walker, D. (2002) 'Managerial power and rent extraction in the design of executive compensation'. *The University of Chicago Law Review*, 69, 751–846, https://doi.org/10.2307/1600632 Bebchuk, L., and Fried, J. (2004) *Pay Without Performance: The Unfulfilled Promise of Executive Compensation*. Cambridge, MA: Harvard University Press.

[33] Frydman, C., and Saks, R. (2010) 'Executive compensation: A new view from a long-term perspective, 1936–2005'. *The Review of Financial Studies*, 23(5), 2099–138,

https://doi.org/10.1093/rfs/hhp120 The managerial power hypothesis can be found in Bebchuk, Fried and Walker (2002) and Bebchuk and Fried (2004).

34 Strictly speaking, there are three order levels to the collective action problem. The first-order collective action problem concerns the costs of collaboration, and the second-order problem concerns the costs of mounting a challenge. There is potentially a third-order collective action problem as well, relating to the cost of enforcement.

35 The median variable pay of a FTSE 100 CEO in 2017 is £3.25 million, according to the CIPD's review of FTSE 100 executive pay published in August 2018. £50 billion is the average UK assets under management of a large investment firm, per the Investment Association's report on asset management in the UK 2017–2018.

36 For data in this section see Mishel and Kandra (2020) and CIPD (2020). For correlation with stock markets indices see Willman, P., and Pepper, A. (2020) 'The role played by large firms in generating income inequality: UK FTSE 100 pay practices in the later twentieth and early twenty-first centuries'. *Economy and Society*, 4(4), 516–39, https://doi.org/10.1080/03085147.2020.1774259

37 £1,000 receivable in three years' time, applying an economic discount for risk and the time value of money of, say, 7 per cent per annum, is worth approximately £800. Applying subjective discount rates of 17 per cent for risk and 33 per cent per annum for time gives a perceived value of around £250. See Pepper, A. (2015) *The Economic Psychology of Incentives*. Basingstoke: Palgrave Macmillan, 59–85.

38 Pepper, A., and Gore, J. (2014) 'The economic psychology of incentives: An international study of top managers'. *Journal of World Business*, 49(3), 350–61, https://doi.org/10.1016/j.jwb.2013.07.002

39 See de Roover, R. (1958) 'The concept of the just price: Theory and economic policy'. *The Journal of Economic History*, 18(4), 418–34, https://doi.org/10.1017/S0022050700107624 Epstein,

S. (1991) 'The theory and practice of the just wage'. *Journal of Medieval History*, 17, 53–69, https://doi.org/10.1016/0304-4181(91)90027-I Also, Fogarty, M. (1961) *The Just Wage*. London: Geoffrey Chapman.

[40] This quotation comes from Book V of *Nichomachean Ethics*, trans. W.D.Ross, cited in Part I of Pojman, L., and McLeod, O. (1999) *What Do We Deserve – A Reader on Justice and Desert*. Oxford and New York: Oxford University Press. The Greek word αξια (*axia*), translated here as 'desert', is sometime alternatively translated as 'worthiness', 'merit', 'value' or 'price'.

[41] Examples of Dworkin's work include Dworkin, R. (1981a) 'What is equality? Part 1: Equality of welfare'. *Philosophy and Public Affairs*, 10(3), 185–246; Dworkin, R. (1981b) 'What is equality? Part 2: Equality of resources'. *Philosophy and Public Affairs*, 10(4), 283–345; Dworkin, R. (2000) *Sovereign Virtue. The Theory and Practice of Equality*. Cambridge, MA: Harvard University Press.

[42] Cohen, G. (2000) *If You're an Egalitarian, How Come You're So Rich?* Cambridge, MA: Harvard University Press. See also Cohen, G. (2008) *Rescuing Justice and Equality*. Cambridge, MA: Harvard University Press.

[43] Frankfurt, H. (1987) 'Equality as a moral ideal'. *Ethics*, 98(1), 21–43, https://doi.org/10.1086/292913

[44] It is worth recording that the difference principle means making the worst-off as well-off as they can be takes priority over any welfare gains to the better-off, no matter how big those welfare gains might be. Some of Rawls's critics have challenged the difference principle on this point.

[45] It is important to note that there is not a one-to-one read across between philosophers and theories. Dworkin and Cohen both support different versions of egalitarianism. On the other hand, it is difficult to find a modern philosopher with whom desert can be uniquely associated.

[46] See de Roover (1958) 'The concept of the just price: Theory and economic policy', 418–34.

[47] Runciman, W. (1966) *Relative Deprivation and Social Justice*. London: Routledge and Kegan Paul.

48 Sources include Rose, D. (2006) 'Social comparisons and so-
    cial order: Issues relating to a possible re-study of W.G. Run-
    ciman's *Relative Deprivation and Social Justice*. *Institute for
    Social and Economic Research Report*, 2006-48; Taylor-Gooby,
    P. (2005) 'Attitudes to social justice'. *Institute for Public Policy
    Research Report*, February.

49 See, for example, an article in *Personnel Today* on 10 May 2021
    about a company called XPO Logistics: 'Logistics giant criti-
    cised for furlough use while paying CEO bonus',
    https://perma.cc/W9JN-M2DX (This was not the only example.)

50 Curtice, J., Hudson, N., and Montagu, I. (eds) (2020) *British
    Social Attitudes: The 37th Report*. London. The National Cen-
    tre for Social Research, https://perma.cc/GD82-XZPA

51 Dworkin would probably not welcome equating 'equality of
    resources' with 'equality of opportunity', of which, he says, 'one
    prominent form holds that people are denied equality when
    their superior position in either welfare or resources is count-
    ed against them in competition for university places or jobs,
    for example' (Dworkin, 1981b, 188). 'Equality of resources' is
    probably, strictly speaking, a subset of 'equality of opportuni-
    ties'. Nevertheless, I have chosen to be less precise in my use
    of terminology, because I think 'equal opportunities' is more
    readily understood than 'equal resources'.

52 Participants were also asked to rank the six principles at soci-
    ety level to help triangulate the results. Society and company
    questions were posed in a different order to minimise the risk
    of order effects.

53 Walzer, M. (1983) *Spheres of Justice – A Defense of Pluralism
    and Equality*. Basic Books, 21.

54 Glen Newey, *Times Literary Supplement*, quoted with reference
    to Miller, D. (1999) *Principles of Social Justice*. Cambridge,
    MA: Harvard University Press.

55 Dewey, J., and Tufts, J. (1908/1932) *Ethics*. Revised Edition.
    New York: Henry Holt and Company, 191.

56 For example, in her book *What's Fair – American Beliefs About
    Distributive Justice*, published in 1981, the Harvard political
    theorist Jennifer Hochschild arranges the five norms of justice

that she identifies ('strict equality', 'need', 'investments', 'results' and 'ascription') along a straight line, from what she describes as the 'principle of equality' at one end of the scale to the 'principle of differentiation' at the other end. Others draw a binary distinction between formalist approaches, for example those associated with Kantian ethics, and utilitarian approaches, associated with Jeremy Bentham and John Stuart Mill – see Schminke, M., Ambrose, M., and Noel, T. (1997) 'The effect of ethical frameworks on perceptions of organizational justice'. *Academy of Management Journal*, 40(5),
https://doi.org/10.5465/256932

[57] The use of field theory in the social sciences was originally pioneered by the social psychologist Kurt Lewin. A field is 'a totality of coexisting facts which are conceived of as mutually interdependent' – see Lewin, K. (1951) *Field Theory in Social Science*. New York: Harper & Brothers, 240. Field theory was made famous by the French sociologist Pierre Bourdieu, who made extensive use of fields in his empirical studies of North African and French society. In the context in which field theory is used in our study, a number of operant factors, including merit, needs and market forces, can be seen at work. Each of these operant factors exerts a force on human beliefs about distributive justice. Conceptualising distributive justice as a field allows a more sophisticated analysis of the different forces at work than the two-dimensional representations of Jennifer Hochschild and others.

[58] Further details can be found in Burri, S., Lup, D., and Pepper, A. (2020) 'What do business executives think about distributive justice?' *Journal of Business Ethics*,
https://doi.org/10.1007/s10551-020-04627-w

[59] See Marshall, G., Swift, A., Routh, D., and Burgoyne, C. (1999) 'What is and what ought to be: Popular beliefs about distributive justice in thirteen countries'. *European Sociological Review*, 15(4), 349–67,
https://doi.org/10.1093/oxfordjournals.esr.a018270

[60] There are two recent intellectual biographies of Rawls: Pogge, T. (2007) *John Rawls – His Life and Theory of Justice*. Oxford:

Oxford University Press; Gališanka, A. (2019) *John Rawls – The Path to a Theory of Justice*. Cambridge, MA: Harvard University Press. See also https://plato.stanford.edu/entries/rawls

61 See, for example, G.A. Cohen's remarks about Rawls in *Rescuing Justice and Equality*, 11–14. Cohen describes Rawls's *A Theory of Justice* as one of the three most important books in Western political philosophy, comparable with Plato's *Republic* and Hobbes's *Leviathan*, in a section entitled 'The Greatness of John Rawls', before starting his extensive critique of Rawls's work.

62 Rawls (1971) *A Theory of Justice*, 60–65.

63 Rawls (1971) *A Theory of Justice*, 78.

64 Frey, D. (2009) *America's Economic Moralists – A History of Rival Ethics and Economics*. Albany, NY: State University of New York Press, 181.

65 Roberts, J. (2010) 'Designing incentives in organizations'. *Journal of Institutional Economics*, 6(1), 125–32, https://doi.org/10.1017/S1744137409990221

66 Frankfurt, H. (2005) *On Bullshit*. Princeton University Press, 16. Originally published in 1986 in *Raritan Quarterly Review*, 6(2), 81–100.

67 Frankfurt, H. (2015) *On Inequality*. Princeton University Press. Originally published in 1987 as 'Equality as a moral ideal' in *Ethics*, 98(1), 21–43, https://doi.org/10.1086/292913

68 Cohen, G. (2008) *Rescuing Justice and Equality*, 32.

69 Cohen, G. (2008) *Rescuing Justice and Equality*, 27. Cohen is quoting from Narveson, J. (1978) 'Rawls on equal distribution of wealth'. *Philosophia*, 7(2), 281–92, https://doi.org/10.1007/BF02378815

70 There is also a huge debate about whether the difference principle applies globally. Rawls argues that the principles of justice only apply to nation states, but this seems somewhat arbitrary, especially when looked at from the perspective of global justice.

71 Cohen, G. (2008) *Rescuing Justice and Equality*, 10.

72 Dworkin, R. (1981a) 'What is equality? Part 1: Equality of welfare'. *Philosophy and Public Affairs*, 10(3), 185–246; Dworkin,

R. (1981b) 'What is equality? Part 2: Equality of resources'. *Philosophy and Public Affairs*, 10(4), 283–345; Dworkin, R. (2000) *Sovereign Virtue*.

[73] Dworkin, R. (1981a) 'What is equality?', 186–7.

[74] Modern economists tend to think of this as a 'no-envy' test; see for example Fleurbaey, M. (2008) *Fairness, Responsibility, and Welfare*. Oxford and New York: Oxford University Press, 21–25.

[75] Dworkin, R. (2003) 'Equality, luck and hierarchy'. *Philosophy and Public Affairs*, 31(2), 190–98, https://doi.org/10.1111/j.1088-4963.2003.00190.x

[76] The Schumpeter column in *The Economist* once put it like this: 'If business had a Moses, "thou shalt link pay to performance" would be on his tablet.' (2021) 'How to design CEO pay to punish iniquity, not just reward virtue', *The Economist*, 20 February, https://perma.cc/TL64-M9JT

[77] Armstrong, M., and Taylor, S. (2003) *Handbook of Human Resource Management Practice*. London: Kogan Page, 4. For more on traditional pay vs. new pay in the context of executive remuneration, see Willman, P., and Pepper, A. (2020) 'The role played by large firms in generating income inequality: UK FTSE 100 pay practices in the late twentieth and early twenty-first centuries'. *Economy and Society*, 49(4), 516–39, https://doi.org/10.1080/03085147.2020.1774259

[78] See Lawler, E. (1990) *Strategic Pay – Aligning Organizational Strategies and Pay Systems*. San Francisco, CA: Jossey-Bass; Schuster, J., and Zingheim, P. (1992) *The New Pay – Linking Employee and Organizational Performance*. San Francisco, CA: Jossey-Bass.

[79] Dworkin, R. (1981a) 'What is equality?'.

[80] This section is indebted to the introduction by Louis Pojman and Owen McLeod to their edited book *What Do We Deserve – A Reader on Justice and Desert*, published in 1999 by Oxford University Press.

[81] Ross, W.D. (1930/2002) *The Right and the Good*. Oxford University Press, cited by Moriarty, J. (2019) 'Desert-based justice'.

In *The Oxford Handbook of Distributive Justice* (ed. Olsaretti, S.). Oxford University Press, 156.

[82] North, D. (1991) 'Institutions'. *Journal of Economic Perspectives*, 5(1), 97–112, https://doi.org/10.1257/jep.5.1.97

[83] Miller, D. (1999) *Principles of Social Justice*. Cambridge, MA: Harvard University Press, 51.

[84] Walzer, M. (1984) *Spheres of Justice*. New York: Basic Books.

[85] Collingwood, R. (1926) 'Economics as a philosophical science'. *Ethics*, 36(2), 174,
https://doi.org/10.1086/intejethi.36.2.2377247

[86] Hayek, F. (1976) 'Social or distributive justice'. In *Law, Legislation, and Liberty*. University of Chicago Press, Volume 2, 80. Hayek quotes R.G Collingwood's essay (1926).

[87] Young, R. (1992) 'Egalitarianism and personal desert'. *Ethics*, 102, 330, https://doi.org/10.1086/293399

[88] Nozick, R. (1974) *Anarchy, State, and Utopia*. Cambridge, MA: Basic Books, 161–3.

[89] Forster, E.M. (1910) *Howards End*. Edward Arnold, cited by Heffer, S. (2017) *The Age of Decadence*, 704.

[90] Gauthier, D. (1986) *Morals By Agreement*. Oxford University Press, 272–3.

[91] The most complete statement of the 'market failures' approach to business ethics is contained in a collection of essays by Joseph Heath, entitled *Morality, Competition, and the Firm*, published by Oxford University Press in 2014. An excellent summary (and partial critique) can be found in Von Kriegstein, H. (2016) 'Professionalism, agency and market failures'. *Business Ethics Quarterly*, 26(4), 445–64,
https://doi.org/10.1017/beq.2016.45

[92] From the *Collected Economic Papers of Joan Robinson* (1979), cited by Boyd, W. (2018) 'Just price, public utility, and the long history of economic regulation in America'. *Yale Journal on Regulation*, 35(3), 721–49,
http://hdl.handle.net/20.500.13051/8274

[93] Cohen, G. (2000) *If You're an Egalitarian, How Come You're So Rich?*, 132.

94 Senge, P. (1990) *The Fifth Discipline – The Art & Practice of the Learning Organization*. Random House, 68–92.

95 Pepper, A. (2006) *Senior Executive Reward – Key Models and Practices*. Gower Publishing, 15. This is a genuine quote from a newspaper article that for various reasons I was not able to cite at the time. Unfortunately, I cannot now find the original source!

96 In Solow, R. (1990) *The Labour Market as a Social Institution*. Oxford: Blackwell. See also Prasch, R. (2004) 'How is labor distinct from broccoli? Unique characteristics of labor and their importance for economic analysis and policy'. In *The Institutionalist Tradition in Labor Economics* (eds Champlin, D., and Knoedler, J.). New York: M.E. Sharpe.

97 Bender, R. (2011) 'Paying for advice: The role of the remuneration consultant in UK listed companies'. *Vanderbilt Law Review*, 64(3), 361–96.

98 An example of an unsuccessful pay cap is found in section 162(m) of the US Internal Revenue Code. This provides that compensation paid to the CEO and the next four highest paid executives in a firm in excess of $1m are not tax deductible unless certain conditions are satisfied. These conditions are that the payments in excess of $1m must be made under a performance-based plan and that the plan must have been approved in advance by shareholders. When this measure was introduced in the US by Congress in 1993 its proponents argued that it would reduce what they regarded as excessive executive compensation by raising the cost to the corporation. It would also, they believed, encourage companies to establish performance-related incentive plans for senior executives. Evidence gathered since the introduction of section 162(m) suggests that the limits on the deductibility of fixed pay over and above the $1m cap led companies to set salaries at or close to the level of the cap and to substantially increase the performance-related components of executive compensation arrangements. The effect on the overall level of executive pay, looked at in terms of companies generally, casts doubt on the effectiveness

of the legislation in constraining executive pay. See, Rose, N., and Wolfram, C. (2000) 'Has the "million-dollar cap" affected CEO pay?' *American Economic Review*, 90(2), 197–202.

[99] See the UK Government's Green Paper (2016) 'Corporate Government Reform', 116. https://perma.cc/R7DG-43KN

[100] Norges Bank Investment Management (2017) 'Remuneration of the CEO – Asset manager perspective', 17 April. https://perma.cc/66YT-SF8G

[101] The Purposeful Company Task Force, a consortium of FTSE companies, investment houses, business schools, business consultancy firms and policymakers, has identified a clear pathway for gaining shareholder approval to restricted stock plans. Replacements to LTIPs are likely to receive shareholder support provided that they adopted the design features specified in their report entitled 'The Purposeful Company Study on Deferred Shares – Progress Review', September 2020, https://perma.cc/V6NL-XBPT

[102] Pepper, A., and Gore, J. (2014) 'The economic psychology of incentives: An international study of top managers'. *Journal of World Business*, 49(3), 350–61, https://doi.org/10.1016/j.jwb.2013.07.002

[103] An important rider to this point is that in November 2021 LGIM announced it was to stop most direct feedback to companies on their executive pay after finding that its responses were often ignored, evidence, perhaps, if any is needed, of the investor's collective action problem – see Agnew, H. (2021) 'LGIM ends feedback on executive pay after finding it mostly ignored', *The Financial Times*, 21 November, https://perma.cc/5F3J-5VY2

[104] The quote by John Cryan comes from Cable, D., and Vermeulen, F. (2016) 'Stop paying executives for performance'. *Harvard Business Review*, 94(2), https://perma.cc/G4BR-MGM7 Support for the idea that extrinsic rewards may crowd out intrinsic motivation can be found in Frey, B. (1997) *Not Just for Money: An Economic Theory of Personal Motivation*. Cheltenham: Edward Elgar Publishing; Frey, B., and Jegen, R. (2001)

'Motivation crowding theory'. *Journal of Economic Surveys*, 15, 589–611, https://doi.org/10.1111/1467-6419.00150 Frey, B., and Oberholzer-Gee, F. (1997) 'The cost of price incentives: An empirical analysis of motivation crowding-out'. *American Economic Review*, 87(4), 746–55; Pepper, A., and Gore, J. (2012) 'Behavioral agency theory: New foundations for theorizing about executive compensation'. *Journal of Management*, 41(4), 1045–68, https://doi.org/10.1177/0149206312461054 Pepper, A., and Gore, J. (2014) 'The economic psychology of incentives: An international study of top managers'. *Journal of World Business*, 49(3), 350–61, https://doi.org/10.1016/j.jwb.2013.07.002

[105] *What Is to Be Done? Burning Questions of Our Movement*, written by Russian revolutionary Vladimir Lenin, was published in 1902 prior to the unsuccessful 1905 revolution.

[106] See https://perma.cc/8BGX-2Q6U

[107] Pizzigati, S. (2018) *The Case for a Maximum Wage*. Polity Press.

[108] See Rose and Wolfram (2000), 197–202; Rose, N., and Wolfram, C. (2002) 'Regulating executive pay: Using the tax code to influence chief executive officer compensation'. *Journal of Labor Economics*, 20(2), 138–75, https://doi.org/10.1086/338677

[109] See McLoughlin, J., and Aizen (2018) 'IRS guidance on 162(m) tax reform', *Harvard Law School Forum on Corporate Governance*, https://perma.cc/HF9S-6PKL

[110] In July 2016, Theresa May, a Conservative, during her successful bid to become UK prime minister, said she would 'get tough on irresponsible behaviour in big business', citing runaway executive pay as creating an 'irrational, unhealthy and growing gap between what these companies pay their workers and what they pay their bosses', although her government failed to follow through on her radical policy agenda. In contrast, in 1998 Peter Mandelson had previously said of the New Labour government that they were 'intensely relaxed about people getting filthy rich', although he did qualify this by also saying 'as long as they pay their taxes'. He subsequently distanced himself from this comment, saying, 'I don't think I'd

say that now'. Sources: Wighton, D. (1998) 'Mandelson plans a microchip off the old block'. *Financial Times*, 23 October; Malik, S. (2012) 'Peter Mandelson gets nervous about people getting "filthy rich"'. *The Guardian*, 26 January, https://perma.cc/PG3R-QQDM Parker, G. (2016) 'Theresa May calls for responsible capitalism in pitch for number 10'. *Financial Times*, 11 July, https://perma.cc/R5GK-YYR2 Walker, O. (2016) 'Theresa May's executive pay plans meet further scepticism'. *Financial Times*, 9 October, https://perma.cc/6GXF-YMSG Davies, R. (2016) 'Theresa May's executive pay reforms challenged by think tank'. *The Guardian*, 25 November, https://perma.cc/V4JN-46RP Lynam, J. (2019) 'Theresa May attacks "unacceptable face of capitalism"'. *BBC News*, 27 August, https://perma.cc/Y5VC-Y5YH

[111] Newell, J. (2013) 'Obama: income inequality is "defining challenge of our time"'. *The Guardian*, 4 December, https://perma.cc/SCB3-553F Weisman, J., and Lublin, J. (2009) 'Obama lays out limits on executive pay'. *The Wall Street Journal*, 5 February, https://perma.cc/4HJK-B5R7 Clark, A. (2010) 'Obama softens stance on Wall Street bonuses'. *The Guardian*, 10 February, https://perma.cc/E5S7-5W22 Hughes, K., and Clarke, T. (2015) 'Trump says high pay for CEOs is "a joke" and "disgraceful"'. Reuters, 13 September, https://perma.cc/K5KU-7GDJ Goodkind, N. (2018) 'Under Trump, CEO pay soars while employee wages decrease – And tax cuts could make gap even bigger'. *Newsweek*, 16 August, https://perma.cc/JEZ3-PGN9 Chalk, N., Keen, M., and Perry, V. (2018) 'The Tax Cuts and Jobs Act: An appraisal' *IMF Working Paper* 18/185, https://perma.cc/B89M-PSBW

[112] Curtice, J., Hudson, N., and Montagu, I. (eds) (2020) *British Social Attitudes: The 37th Report*. London. The National Centre for Social Research. https://perma.cc/AN2C-CQ3K

[113] The various sources for this and the earlier paragraphs in this section include Bannock, G., Baxter, R., and Davis, E. (1972/2003) *Dictionary of Economics. The Economist* in

association with Profile Books Ltd; Proudfoot, M. and Lacey, A. (2010) *The Routledge Dictionary of Philosophy*. Routledge Taylor & Francis; Russell, B. (2013) 'Ethical axions', Chapter 7 in *Russell on Ethics* (ed., Pigden, C.). Routledge Taylor & Francis; Moore, G.E. (1929) *Principia Ethica*. Cambridge University Press; Perry, R. (1916) 'Economic and moral value'. *The Quarterly Journal of Economics*, 30(3), 443–85, https://doi.org/10.2307/1885234 Masconale, S., and Sepe, S. (2021) 'Corporate conformism'. *European Corporate Governance Institute Working Paper* 568/2021 March, https://perma.cc/8FUG-5SPY

[114] See the legal opinion provided by global law firm Freshfields Bruckhaus Deringer, entitled *Framework for the Integration of Environmental, Social and Governance Issues into Institutional Investment: A Report Produced for the Asset Management Working Group of the UN Environment Programme Finance Initiative*, published in 2005, https://perma.cc/3AXZ-FHYR

[115] *Fiduciary Duties of Investment Intermediaries*, published by the Law Commission of England and Wales, 1 July 2014, https://perma.cc/HD5J-BDQU

[116] But see endnote 103 above.

[117] Principal data sources: Income Data Services, for 2000–2015. CIPD Executive Pay in the FTSE 100 annual reviews for 2016–2020.

[118] The source of US pay data is Mishel, L., and Wolfe, J. (2019) 'CEO compensation has grown 940% since 1978'. Report published by the Economic Policy Institute, https://perma.cc/9F7R-X8LP

[119] Flood, C. (2020) 'Larry Fink retains position as highest paid CEO in asset management', *Financial Times*, 15 August, https://perma.cc/2CH9-RQHP

[120] Elizabeth Anscombe's seminal essay on virtue ethics, entitled 'Modern moral philosophy', was published in 1958 in *Philosophy*, 33, 1–9. See also Foot, P. (1978) *Virtues and Vices*. Oxford: Blackwell; MacIntyre, A. (1985) *After Virtue*. London: Duckworth.

[121] 'Fairness in business', a report published by A Blueprint for a Better Business in conjunction with the RSA in 2019, https://perma.cc/3N8P-TPBL See also Confino, J. (2014) 'Society must call business' bluff on its fixation with profit maximisation'. *The Guardian*, 5 November, https://perma.cc/G72A-H6ZD

[122] Kay, J. (2012) *The Kay Review of UK Equity Markets and Long-Term Decision Making*, published under the 2010–2015 Conservative and Liberal Democrat government, https://perma.cc/AKY2-RW7M

[123] Mark Twain's historical novel *The Prince and the Pauper* (1881) tells the story of Tom Canty, youngest member of a poor family in 16th-century London, who changes places with Edward Tudor, Prince of Wales. Though written for children, the tale is a critique of extreme wealth and income inequality.

[124] A third of WPP shareholders voted against Martin Sorrell's £70m pay for 2015, branding it as 'excessive' and 'unacceptable' – see Williams, H. and William, H. (2017), 'Third of Shareholders Rebel over WPP Chief Sir Martin Sorrell's £70m Pay Deal'. *Huffington Post* (9 June), https://perma.cc/XP4F-PLCX In an FT Investigation, Madison Marriage and Matthew Garrahan commented on the size of Sorrell's benefits and expense allowances, as well the extraordinary pay-out of £70m which sparked an investor revolt – see 'Martin Sorrell's downfall: why the ad king left WPP', *Financial Times*, 11 June 2018, https://perma.cc/XQX6-XMT9 Guardian columnist Nick Cohen cited Martin Sorrell's pay in an article entitled 'Executive greed is still a besetting sin'. *The Guardian*, 30 October 2011, https://perma.cc/JY2K-RBGU Martin Vander Weyer provides a more nuanced view on Martin Sorrell's pay in chapter 7, Vander Meyer, M. (2021) *The Good, The Bad, and The Greedy: Why We've Lost Faith in Capitalism*. Biteback Publishing.

[125] Karl Popper's work on natural laws and the falsification principle is found in *The Logic of Scientific Discovery*, first published in German as *Logik der Forschung* in 1935. Juvenal wrote in Satire VI about '*rara avis in terris nigroque simillima cygno*' ('a

rare bird in the lands and very much like a black swan'). Data about the world's swan population come from Rees, E., et al (2019) 'Conservation status of the world's swan populations, Cygnus sp. and Coscoroba sp.: a review of current trends and gaps in knowledge'. *Wildfowl*, Special Issue 5, 35–72.

[126] Kerr, J. (2013) *Legacy – What the All Blacks Can Teach Us About the Business of Life*. London: Constable & Robinson.

[127] The postscript draws heavily on Leeson, P. (2007) 'The law and economics of pirate organisation'. *Journal of Political Economy*, 115(6), 1049–94, https://doi.org/10.1086/526403 also Rediker, M. (1987) *Between the Devil and the Deep Blue Sea: Merchant Ships, Pirates and the Anglo-American Maritime World, 1700–1750*. Cambridge University Press; Woodward, C. (2007) *The Republic of Pirates*. Orlando, FL: Harcourt.

[128] A 'piece of eight' was ⅛ of an ounce of silver, which was worth perhaps $1 at the beginning of the 18th century or $21 in 2020 after accounting for inflation. So 600 pieces of eight would have been worth around $1,575 in 2020 terms – not, it has to be said, a great deal of money to compensate for the loss of a leg.

[129] For further reading, see Appiah, K. (2008) *Experiments in Ethics (Flexner Lectures)*. Harvard University Press.

References

Appiah, K. (2008) *Experiments in Ethics (Flexner Lectures)*. Cambridge, MA: Harvard University Press.

Anscombe, E. (1958) 'Modern moral philosophy'. *Philosophy*, 33, 1–9.

Bebchuk, L., and Fried, J. (2004) *Pay Without Performance – The Unfulfilled Promise of Executive Compensation*. Cambridge, MA: Harvard University Press.

Burri, S., Lup, D., and Pepper, A. (2021) 'What do business executives think about distributive justice?' *Journal of Business Ethics*, 174(1), 13–33. https://doi.org/10.1007/s10551-020-04627-w

Cohen, G. (2000) *If You're an Egalitarian, How Come You're so Rich?* Cambridge, MA: Harvard University Press.

Cohen, G. (2008) *Rescuing Justice and Equality*. Cambridge, MA: Harvard University Press.

Davis, G. (2009) *Managed by Markets: How Finance Re-shaped America*. Oxford and New York: Oxford University Press.

Dworkin, R. (2000) *Sovereign Virtue. The Theory and Practice of Equality*. Cambridge, MA: Harvard University Press.

Fleurbaey, M. (2008) *Fairness, Responsibility, and Welfare*. Oxford and New York: Oxford University Press.

Fogarty, M. (1961) *The Just Wage*. London: Geoffrey Chapman.

Foot, P. (1978) *Virtues and Vices and Other Essays in Moral Philosophy*. Oxford. Blackwell.

Frankfurt, H. (1987) 'Equality as a moral ideal'. *Ethics*, 98(1), 21–43.

Frey, B. (1997) *Not Just for Money: An Economic Theory of Personal Motivation*. Cheltenham: Edward Elgar Publishing.

Frey, D. (2009) *America's Economic Moralists – A History of Rival Ethics and Economics*. Albany, NY: State University of New York Press

Friedman, M. (1970) 'The social responsibility of business is to increase its profits'. *New York Times Magazine*, 13 September.

Frydman, C., and Saks, R. (2010) 'Executive compensation: a new view from a long-term perspective, 1936-2005.' *The Review of Financial Studies,* 23(5) pp. 2099–2138. https://doi.org/10.1093/rfs/hhp120

Gauthier, D. (1986) *Morals By Agreement*. Oxford University Press.

Hayek, F. (1976) 'Social or distributive justice'. In *Law, Legislation, and Liberty*. Chicago, IL: University of Chicago Press, Volume 2, 80.

Heath, J. (2014) *Morality, Competition, and the Firm*. New York: Oxford University Press.

Heffer, S. (2017) *The Age of Decadence: Britain 1880 to 1914*. Random House Books.

Hochschild, J. (1981) *What's Fair – American Beliefs about Distributive Justice*. Cambridge, MA: Harvard University Press.

Jensen, M., and Meckling, W. (1976) 'Theory of the firm: Managerial behavior, agency costs and ownership structure'. *Journal of Financial Economics*, 3(4), 305–60. https://doi.org/10.1016/0304-405X(76)90026-X

Kamm, F. (2016) *The Trolley Problem Mysteries. The Berkeley Tanner Lectures*. New York: Oxford University Press.

Kerr, J. (2013) *Legacy – What the All Blacks Can Teach Us About the Business of Life*. London: Constable & Robinson.

Krippner, G. (2012) *Capitalizing on Crisis – The Political Origins of the Rise of Finance*. Cambridge, MA: Harvard University Press.

Lawler, E. (1990) *Strategic Pay – Aligning Organizational Strategies and Pay Systems*. San Francisco, CA: Jossey-Bass.

Leeson, P. (2007) 'The law and economics of pirate organization'. *Journal of Political Economy*, 115(6), 1049–94. https://doi.org/10.1086/526403.

Lenin, V. (1902/1963) *What Is to Be Done? Burning Questions of Our Movement*. Oxford University Press.

Lewin, K. (1951) *Field Theory in Social Science*. New York: Harper & Brothers.

MacIntyre, A. (1981) *After Virtue – A Study in Moral Theory*. University of Notre Dame Press.

Miller, D. (1999) *Principles of Social Justice*. Cambridge, MA: Harvard University Press.

Misak, C. (2013) *The American Pragmatists*. Oxford: Oxford University Press.

Narveson, J. (1978) 'Rawls on equal distribution of wealth'. *Philosophia*, 7(2), 281–92. https://doi.org/10.1007/BF02378815

Moore, G. (1929) *Principia Ethica*. Cambridge University Press.

Nozick, R. (1974) *Anarchy, State, and Utopia*. Cambridge, MA: Basic Books.

Olsaretti, S. (2019) *The Oxford Handbook of Distributive Justice*. Oxford: Oxford University Press.

Pepper, A. (2006) *Senior Executive Reward – Key Models and Practices*. Aldershot: Gower Publishing.

Pepper, A. (2015) *The Economic Psychology of Incentives – New Design Principles for Executive Pay*. Basingstoke: Palgrave Macmillan.

Piketty, T. (2014) *Capital in the Twenty-First Century*. Cambridge, MA: The Belknap Press of Harvard University Press.

Pizzigati, S. (2018) *The Case for a Maximum Wage*. Cambridge: Polity Press.

Pojman, L., and McLeod, O. (1999) *What Do We Deserve – A Reader on Justice and Desert*. Oxford and New York: Oxford University Press.

Popper, K. (1935/2002). *Logik der Forschung* [*The Logic of Scientific Discovery*]. London and New York: Routledge Classics.

Rawls, J. (1971/1999). *A Theory of Justice*. Oxford University Press.

Ross, W.D. (1930/2002) *The Right and the Good*. Oxford: Oxford University Press.

Rediker, M (1987) *Between the Devil and the Deep Blue Sea: Merchant Ships, Pirates and the Anglo-American Maritime World, 1700–1750*. Cambridge: Cambridge University Press.

Russell, B. (1999) *Russell on Ethics* (ed. Pigden, C.). Routledge Taylor & Francis.

Schuster, J., and Zingheim, P. (1992) *The New Pay – Linking Employee and Organizational Performance*. San Francisco, CA: Jossey-Bass.

Solow, R. (2017) 'Thomas Piketty is right'. In *After Piketty – The Agenda for Economics and Inequality* (eds Boushey, H., Delong, J.B., and Steinbaum, M.). Cambridge, MA: Harvard University Press, 48–59.

Toulmin, S. (1950) *The Place of Reason in Ethics*. Cambridge University Press.

Twain, M., and Warner, C. (1873) *The Gilded Age: A Tale of Today*. American Publishing Company.

Willman, P., and Pepper, A. (2020) 'The role played by large firms in generating income inequality: UK FTSE 100 pay practices in the later twentieth and early twenty-first centuries'. *Economy and Society*, 4(4), 516–39.
https://doi.org/10.1080/03085147.2020.1774259

Woodward, C. (2007) *The Republic of Pirates*. Orlando, FL: Harcourt.

Lightning Source UK Ltd.
Milton Keynes UK
UKHW021829151122
412263UK00010B/124